Blood

by Lars Norén

Translated by Maja Zade

Methuen Drama

Published by Methuen 2003

1 3 5 7 9 10 8 6 4 2

First published as *Blod* in 1996 by
Rowohlt Taschenbuch Verlag GmbH,
Reinbek bei Hamburg

Methuen Publishing Limited Reg. No. 3543167

A CIP catalogue record for this book is available from the British Library.

ISBN 0 413 77404 X

Typeset by SX Composing
Printed and bound in Great Britain by
Cox and Wyman Ltd, Reading, Berkshire

Caution
All rights in this play are strictly reserved.
Application for performance, etc., should be made before rehearsals
begin to: Corinna Brocher, Rowohlt Theater Verlag, Hamburger
Straße 17, Reinbek bei Hamburg 21465, Germany.

Lars Norén was born in Stockholm in 1944. He is one of Scandinavia's most prolific playwrights and is currently Artistic Director of Riks Drama at Riksteatern, Stockholm. He started writing at the age of thirteen and has published three novels as well as poetry. A selection of his stage plays includes *Natten är dagens mor* ('Night, Mother of the Day', Malmö, Stadsteater, 1982); *Smiles of the Inferno* (Det Kongelige Teater, Copenhagen, 1982); *Demoner* ('Demons', Stadsteater, Stockholm, 1984); *Munich–Athens* (Café Teatret, Copenhagen, 1986); *Autumn and Winter* (Café Teatret, Copenhagen, 1989); *And Give Us The Shadows* (Det Norske Teater, Oslo, 1991); *The Clinic* (Plaza Theatre, Stockholm, 1996); *Ett Sorts Hades* ('A Kind of Hades', Toneelgroep Amsterdam, 1997); *Romanians* (Plaza Theatre, Stockholm, 1997); Skuggpojkarna ('Shadowboys' Dramaten/Riksteatern, Stockholm, 1999) and *November* (Der Norske Teatret, Oslo, 2001). He has also worked extensively on TV and Radio

BLOOD

by **Lars Norén**

Translated by Maja Zade

Cast in order of appearance
Rosa **Francesca Annis**
Madeleine H **Ingrid Lacey**
Eric **Nicholas Le Prevost**
Luca **Tom Hardy**

Director **James Macdonald**
Designer **Hildegard Bechtler**
Lighting Designer **Peter Mumford**
Associate Lighting Designer **Rachael McCutcheon**
Sound Designer **Ian Dickinson**
Assistant Director **Tiffany Watt-Smith**
Assistant to Designer **Karoline Weber**
Casting **Lisa Makin, Amy Ball**
Production Manager **Paul Handley**
Stage Manager **Cath Binks**
Deputy Stage Manager **Tinky Walker**
Assistant Stage Manager **Fay Mansfield**
Costume Supervisor **Iona Kenrick**
Costume Assistant **Georgina Turcan**
Props & Furniture Buyers **Lisa Buckley, Kathy Anders**
Set built by **Scott Fleary Ltd., Weld Fab Stage Engineering Ltd.**

The Royal Court Theatre would like to thank the following for their help with this production:
The Embassy of Sweden and The Swedish Institute, Perrine Desproges, Peter Drury from Amnesty
International, Mariano Fernandez Chilean Ambassador, Patricio Guzman, Terence Higgins Trust, Teresa
Salazar-Hope, Cleo van Velsern.

THE COMPANY

Lars Norén (writer)

For the Royal Court: November (Nordic Readings 2002).

Other theatre includes: Under, Kyla, Kommer och försvinner, Sju Tre (Riksteatern, Stockholm); Tyst Musik (Riksteatern/Stadsteatern, Stockholm); Akt (Riksteatern, Stockholm/Theatre de Liége, Belgium); Fursteslickaren (Lilla Scen, Stockholm); Depressionen, Dräneringen, När de brände fjärilar på lilla scenen; Modet att döda (Swedish radio); Orestes, Sommar, Tiden är vårt hem (Dramaten, Stockholm); En fruktansvärd lycka (Stockholms Stadsteater); München - Aten (Cafe Teatret, Copenhagen); Underjordens leende (Det Kongelige Teater, Copenhagen); Natten är dagens mor (Malmö Stadsteater/Theater Basel); Kaos är granne med Gud (Göteborgs Stadsteater); Demoner (Stockholms Stadsteater/Schauspielhaus Bochum); Hämndaria (Upsalsa Stadsteater/Staatsheater Darmstadt); Vilstolen/Aska (Teatret ved Sorte Hest, Copenhagen); Nattvarden (Dramaten, Stockholm/ Schauspielhaus Bochum); Stillheten (Het Publiekstheater, Amsterdam); Komedianterna/ Sorgespelet (Swedish televison); Endagsvarelser (Staastheater Kassel); Hebriana (Het Nationale Toneel, Dan Haag); Höst och vinter (Cafe Teatret, Copenhagen/Bremer Theater); Bobby Fischer bor i Pasadena (Swedish television/Staatstheater Wiesbaden); Och ge oss skuggorna (Det Norske Teater, Oslo/Städtische Bühnen Münster); Sanning och konsekens (Swedish television); Så enkel är kärleken (Theater de Appel, Den Haag); Löven i Vallombrosa (Schauspiel Bonn); Rumäner (Plaza Theater, Stockholm/Schauspiel Bonn); Blod (Betty Nansen Teatret, Copenhagen/Theater Oberhausen); Trio till tidens ände (Swedish radio); Ett sorts Hades (Toneelgroep Amsterdam/Staatstheater Kassel); Kliniken (Plaza Theater, Stockholm/Schauspielhaus Zürich); Personkrets 3:1 – Morire di Classe (Schaubühne am Lehniner Platz, Berlin); Skuggpojkarna (Dramaten (Elverket)/Riksteatern, Stockholm/Bühnen der Stadt Köln); November (Det Norske Teatret, Oslo/Staatstheater Stuttgart); Tristano (Deutches Theater Berlin); Stilla Vatten (Riksteatern/Judiska Teatern, Stockholm); Detajler (Dramaten/Det Kongelige Theater Copenhagen).

Francesca Annis

Theatre includes: The Vortex (Donmar); Ghosts (Windsor/West End); Hamlet (London/US tour); The Heretic (London Stage); Arms and the Man (Windsor); Romeo and Juliet, Troilus and Cressida (RSC); Month in the Country (RNT); Three Sisters (Albery); Mrs Klein (RNT/Apollo); Sienna Red (UK tour); Rosmersholm (Young Vic); Lady Windermere's Fan (tour & West End); Hedda Gabler (Plymouth tour).

Television includes: Schumann, The Family is a Vicious Circle, Once Upon a Time, The Chinese Prime Minister, Peer Gynt, A Pin to See the Peep Show, Death of an Old-fashioned Girl, Edward VI I, The Couch, The Wood Demon, Madame Bovary, The Way of the World, Comedy of Errors, Caversbridge, The Ragazza, Lillie, Why Didn't They Ask Evans, Partners in Crime, The Secret Adversary, Shades of Darkness - The Maze, Magnum P.I - Deja Vu, Inside Story, Ari, Haunting Harmony, Parnell, Absolute Hell, Gravy Train I I, Weep No More My Lady, Headhunters, Between the Lines, Dalziel and Pascoe, Tales from the Crypt, Reckless, Deadly Summer, Wives and Daughters, Deceit.

Film includes: Copenhagen, Debt Collector, The Walking Stick, Macbeth, Big Mack & Poor Clare, Penny Gold, Gemini, Coming out of the Ice, Krull, Dune, El Rio de Oro, Under the Cherry Moon, Milk.

Hildegard Bechtler (designer)

For the Royal Court: Terrorism, Blasted, The Changing Room.

Other theatre includes: The Master Builder (Albery); The Merchant of Venice, King Lear (RNT); La Maison de la Puppée (Theatre de l'Europe, Paris); Footfalls (Garrick); The St. Pancras Project (LIFT); Richard II (RNT/ Bobigny, Paris); Electra (RSC/Riverside/ Bobigny, Paris); Hedda Gabler (Abbey, Dublin/Playhouse, London); Coriolanus (Salzburg Festival).

Film and television includes: The Merchant of Venice, Richard II, The Wasteland, Hedda Gabler, Coming Up Roses, Business As Usual.

Opera includes: The Ring Cycle: Das Rheingold, Walküre, Siegfried and Götterdämmerung, (Scottish Opera/Edinburgh Festival); Lady Macbeth of Mtsensk (Sydney Opera House); Paul Bunyan (ROH); War & Peace, Boris Gudonov, Peter Grimes, Lohengrin, The Bacchae (ENO); Dialogues Des Carmelites (Japan/Paris Opera);

Simon Boccanegra, Peter Grimes (Staatsoper, Munich); Don Carlos, Wozzeck, Katya Kabanova (Opera North); Don Giovanni (Glyndebourne); La Wally (Bregenz Festival/ Amsterdam Musik Theatre).

Ian Dickinson (sound designer)
For the Royal Court: Playing the Victim, Fallout, Flesh Wound, Hitchcock Blonde (& Lyric), Black Milk, Crazyblackmuthafuckin'self, Caryl Churchill Shorts, Imprint, Mother Teresa is Dead, Push Up, Workers Writes, Fucking Games, Herons, Cutting Through the Carnival.
Other theatre includes: Port (Royal Exchange Manchester); Night of the Soul (RSC Barbican); Eyes of the Kappa (Gate); Crime and Punishment in Dalston (Arcola Theatre); Search and Destroy (New End, Hampstead); Phaedra, Three Sisters, The Shaughraun, Writer's Cramp (Royal Lyceum, Edinburgh); The Whore's Dream (RSC Fringe, Edinburgh); As You Like It, An Experienced Woman Gives Advice, Present Laughter, The Philadelphia Story, Wolks World, Poor Superman, Martin Yesterday, Fast Food, Coyote Ugly, Prizenight (Royal Exchange, Manchester).
Ian is Head of Sound at the Royal Court.

Tom Hardy
Theatre includes: The Modernists (Sheffield Crucible); In Arabia We'd All Be Kings (Hampstead).
Television includes: Band of Brothers.
Film includes: Layer Cake, LD50, Dot The I, Star Trek: Nemesis, Simon, Black Hawk Down, The Reckoning.

Ingrid Lacey
For the Royal Court: Our Late Night.
Other theatre includes: Gone to LA (Hampstead); After the Rain (Gate).
Television includes: Bedtime, The Last Detective, Casualty, Heartbeat, Getting Hurt, Drop the Dead Donkey, Master of the Moor, The Chief, A Woman's Guide to Adultery, White Girls on Dope, Strathblair, Dream Kitchen, Never Come Back, Saracen, London's Burning, The Endless Game, Inspector Morse, Northanger Abbey, Thunder Rock.
Film includes: The Cat's Meow, In Love and War.

Nicholas Le Prevost
For the Royal Court: The Glad Hand, The Last Supper, Seven Lears, Victory, Golgo, Eastern Promise (Mayday Festival), The Strip.
Other theatre includes: Where There's a Will (tour); Mozart's Impresario (Barbican); Much Ado About Nothing (RSC/Theatre Royal Haymarket/ London/ Newcastle); My Fair Lady (RNT/Drury Lane); Last Dance at Dum Dum (Ambassadors); As You Like It (Crucible, Sheffield/Lyric, Hammersmith); Amadeus (Old Vic); The Recruiting Officer, Hedda Gabler (Chichester Festival Theatre); Privates on Parade (Greenwich/tour); The Prime of Miss Jean Brodie (RNT); An Absolute Turkey (Gielgud).
Television includes: Foyle's War, Fortysomething, My Dad's the Prime Minister, The King's Servant, The End of the Law, Midsomer Murders, Inspector Morse, Harnessing Peacocks, Jewel in the Crown, It Takes a Worried Man, The Borgias, The Imitation Game, Stolen, The Great Paperchase, The Camomile Lawn, Up the Garden Path, The Vicar of Dibley.
Film includes: Bright Young Things, Gladiatress, Being Considered, Shakespeare in Love, Cold Enough for Snow, Land Girls, Letters from the East, Clockwise.

James Macdonald (director)
Associate Director of the Royal Court since 1992. Currently on a NESTA Fellowship.
For the Royal Court: Blasted, 4.48 Psychosis, Hard Fruit, Real Classy Affair, Cleansed, Bailegangaire, Harry and Me, The Changing Room, Simpatico, Peaches, Thyestes, The Terrible Voice of Satan, Hammett's Apprentice, Putting Two and Two Together.
Other theatre includes: Die Kopien (Berlin Schaubühne); 4.48 Psychose (Vienna Burgtheater); The Tempest, Roberto Zucco (RSC); The Triumph of Love (Almeida); Love's Labour's Lost, Richard II (Manchester Royal Exchange); The Rivals (Nottingham Playhouse); The Crackwalker (Gate); The Seagull (Sheffield Crucible); Neon Gravy (RNT Studio); Miss Julie (Oldham Coliseum); Juno and the Paycock, Ice Cream & Hot Fudge, Romeo and Juliet, Fool for Love, Savage/Love, Master Harold and the Boys (Contact Theatre); Prem (BAC, Soho Poly).
Opera includes: Rigoletto (WNO); Die Zauberflöte (Garsington); Wolf Club Village; Night Banquet (Almeida Opera); Oedipus Rex; Survivor from Warsaw (Royal Exchange/Halle); Lives of the Great Poisoners (Second Stride).

Rachael McCutcheon (associate lighting designer)
As assistant designer, theatre includes: Coast of Utopia, Love's Labour's Lost (RNT), Anything Goes (RNT/Drury Lane).
Opera includes: Siegfried and Götterdämmerung (Scottish Opera's Ring Cycle).
As designer, theatre includes: Outside on the Street (Gate).
Opera includes: projects with Scottish Opera and Opera North.
Dance includes: Footsteps Dance Company (New Zealand tour).

Peter Mumford (lighting designer)
For the Royal Court: The People are Friendly, Redundant.
Other theatre includes: Brand (RSC Swan/ Theatre Royal Haymarket); Betrayal, Design for Living, Fight for Barbara, As You Like It (Theatre Royal, Bath); The Talking Cure, Bacchai, Summerfolk, The Merchant of Venice, Money, The Prime of Miss Jean Brodie, Luther (RNT); Private Lives (Albery/Broadway); Hamlet (RSC/Barbican); Iphigenia (Abbey, Dublin); God Only Knows (Vaudeville); Medea (Queen's); The Dispute & The Critic (Royal Exchange, Manchester); Lautrec (Shaftesbury Avenue); Othello, The Taming of the Shrew (RSC); A Long Day's Journey into Night, An Ideal Husband, Oliver Twist, Therese Raquin (Gate, Dublin).
Film and television includes: directing Forty-Eight Preludes and Fugues (BBC2), Director of Photography for Jenufa.
Opera includes: L'Heure Espagnole, Les Enfants et Les Sortileges (lit, co-directed and designed for Opera Zuid, Holland); La Traviata (Antwerp Opera); Siegfried and Götterdämerung (Scottish Opera/Edinburgh Festival); The Bartered Bride (ROH); Il Corsaro (Athens Concert Hall); Don Pasquale (Opera Zuid, Holland);
The Coronation of Poppea (ENO); I Laskarina (Acropol Theatre, Athens); Eugene Onegin, Madame Butterfly (Opera North); Giulio Cesare (Opera de Bordeaux); Earth and the Great Weather (directed and designed, Almeida Opera 2000); Un Ballo In Maschera (also designed for Vilnius Festival/Opera House).
Dance includes: Madame Butterfly (Northern Ballet); Of Oil and Water (Siobhan Davies Dance Co.); Irek Mukhamedov and Dancers (Sadler's Wells); Arthur (Birmingham Royal Ballet); The Crucible, Hidden Variables, A Stranger's Taste, This House Will Burn (Royal Ballet); Sounding, Unrest, The Celebrated Soubrette (Rambert Dance Co.).
Awards include: 2003 Laurence Olivier Award for Best Lighting Design for Bacchai, Best Lighting Designer for Iphigenia at The Irish Theatre Awards, 1995 Laurence Olivier Award for Outstanding Achievement in Dance for The Glass Blew In and Fearful Symmetries and was nominated for Best Lighting Designer in 2000 and 2002.

Tiffany Watt-Smith (assistant director)
Tiffany is Associate Director at Arcola Theatre.
As assistant director, theatre includes: Coriolanus (RSC Swan).
As director, theatre includes: Kismet, Mud, Venezuala, Trash, Teatro X La Identidad (Arcola Theatre).
Tiffany also works as a freelance writer for film and television.

Karoline Weber (assistant to the designer)
As assistant designer: The Elephant Vanishes (Complicite); Ein Fest für Boris (Berliner Ensemble); Ballata (Theatre de la Monnaie, Brussels); Eine Unbekannte aus der Seine (Schaubühne am Lehniner Platz, Berlin).
As designer: Buffa (Pipe Dream Company, Hoxton Hall); La Scatola (Kulturbrauerei, Berlin/Teatro Grecco, Rome).

Maja Zade (translator)
Translations for the Royal Court: Push Up, Fireface, Parasites.
Other translations include: God is a DJ, The Cold Child as well as translations from German and Swedish for the Royal Court International Residency.
Maja Zade is currently dramaturg at the Schaubühne am Lehniner Platz in Berlin.

THE ENGLISH STAGE COMPANY AT THE ROYAL COURT

The English Stage Company at the Royal Court opened in 1956 as a subsidised theatre producing new British plays, international plays and some classical revivals.

The first artistic director George Devine aimed to create a writers' theatre, 'a place where the dramatist is acknowledged as the fundamental creative force in the theatre and where the play is more important than the actors, the director, the designer'. The urgent need was to find a contemporary style in which the play, the acting, direction and design are all combined. He believed that 'the battle will be a long one to continue to create the right conditions for writers to work in'.

Devine aimed to discover 'hard-hitting, uncompromising writers whose plays are stimulating, provocative and exciting'. The Royal Court production of John Osborne's Look Back in Anger in May 1956 is now seen as the decisive starting point of modern British drama and the policy created a new generation of British playwrights. The first wave included John Osborne, Arnold Wesker, John Arden, Ann Jellicoe, N F Simpson and Edward Bond. Early seasons included new international plays by Bertolt Brecht, Eugène Ionesco, Samuel Beckett, Jean-Paul Sartre and Marguerite Duras.

The theatre started with the 400-seat proscenium arch Theatre Downstairs, and then in 1969 opened a second theatre, the 60-seat studio Theatre Upstairs. Some productions transfer to the West End, such as Terry Johnson's Hitchcock Blonde, Caryl Churchill's Far Away, Conor McPherson's The Weir, Kevin Elyot's Mouth to Mouth and My Night With Reg. The Royal Court also co-produces plays which have transferred to the West End or toured internationally, such as Sebastian Barry's The Steward of Christendom and Mark Ravenhill's Shopping and Fucking (with Out of Joint), Martin McDonagh's The Beauty Queen Of Leenane (with Druid Theatre Company), Ayub Khan-Din's East is East (with Tamasha Theatre Company, and now a feature film).

Since 1994 the Royal Court's artistic policy has again been vigorously directed to finding and producing a new generation of playwrights. The writers include Joe Penhall, Rebecca Prichard, Michael Wynne, Nick Grosso, Judy Upton, Meredith Oakes, Sarah Kane, Anthony Neilson, Judith Johnson, James Stock, Jez Butterworth, Marina Carr, Phyllis Nagy, Simon Block, Martin McDonagh, Mark Ravenhill, Ayub Khan-Din, Tamantha Hammerschlag, Jess Walters, Ché Walker, Conor McPherson, Simon Stephens,

photo: Andy Chopping

Richard Bean, Roy Williams, Gary Mitchell, Mick Mahoney, Rebecca Gilman, Christopher Shinn, Kia Corthron, David Gieselmann, Marius von Mayenburg, David Eldridge, Leo Butler, Zinnie Harris, Grae Cleugh, Roland Schimmelpfennig, DeObia Oparei, Vassily Sigarev and the Presnyakov Brothers. This expanded programme of new plays has been made possible through the support of A.S.K Theater Projects and the Skirball Foundation, the Jerwood Charitable Foundation, the American Friends of the Royal Court Theatre and many of the plays presented in association with the Royal National Theatre Studio.

In recent years there have been record-breaking productions at the box office, with capacity houses for Roy Williams' Fallout, Terry Johnson's Hitchcock Blonde, Caryl Churchill's A Number, Jez Butterworth's The Night Heron, Rebecca Gilman's Boy Gets Girl, Kevin Elyot's Mouth To Mouth, David Hare's My Zinc Bed and Conor McPherson's The Weir, which transferred to the West End in October 1998 and ran for nearly two years at the Duke of York's Theatre.

The newly refurbished theatre in Sloane Square opened in February 2000, with a policy still inspired by the first artistic director George Devine. The Royal Court is an international theatre for new plays and new playwrights, and the work shapes contemporary drama in Britain and overseas.

AWARDS FOR THE ROYAL COURT

Jez Butterworth won the 1995 George Devine Award, the Writers' Guild New Writer of the Year Award, the Evening Standard Award for Most Promising Playwright and the Olivier Award for Best Comedy for Mojo.

The Royal Court was the overall winner of the 1995 Prudential Award for the Arts for creativity, excellence, innovation and accessibility. The Royal Court Theatre Upstairs won the 1995 Peter Brook Empty Space Award for innovation and excellence in theatre.

Michael Wynne won the 1996 Meyer-Whitworth Award for The Knocky. Martin McDonagh won the 1996 George Devine Award, the 1996 Writers' Guild Best Fringe Play Award, the 1996 Critics' Circle Award and the 1996 Evening Standard Award for Most Promising Playwright for The Beauty Queen of Leenane. Marina Carr won the 19th Susan Smith Blackburn Prize (1996/7) for Portia Coughlan. Conor McPherson won the 1997 George Devine Award, the 1997 Critics' Circle Award and the 1997 Evening Standard Award for Most Promising Playwright for The Weir. Ayub Khan-Din won the 1997 Writers' Guild Awards for Best West End Play and Writers' Guild New Writer of the Year and the 1996 John Whiting Award for East is East (co-production with Tamasha).

At the 1998 Tony Awards, Martin McDonagh's The Beauty Queen of Leenane (co-production with Druid Theatre Company) won four awards including Garry Hynes for Best Director and was nominated for a further two. Eugene Ionesco's The Chairs (co-production with Theatre de Complicite) was nominated for six Tony awards. David Hare won the 1998 Time Out Live Award for Outstanding Achievement and six awards in New York including the Drama League, Drama Desk and New York Critics Circle Award for Via Dolorosa. Sarah Kane won the 1998 Arts Foundation Fellowship in Playwriting. Rebecca Prichard won the 1998 Critics' Circle Award for Most Promising Playwright for Yard Gal (co-production with Clean Break).

Conor McPherson won the 1999 Olivier Award for Best New Play for The Weir. The Royal Court won the 1999 ITI Award for Excellence in International Theatre. Sarah Kane's Cleansed was judged Best Foreign Language Play in 1999 by Theater Heute in Germany. Gary Mitchell won the 1999 Pearson Best Play Award for Trust. Rebecca Gilman was joint winner of the 1999 George Devine Award and won the 1999 Evening Standard Award for Most Promising Playwright for The Glory of Living.

In 1999, the Royal Court won the European theatre prize New Theatrical Realities, presented at Taormina Arte in Sicily, for its efforts in recent years in discovering and producing the work of young British dramatists.

Roy Williams and Gary Mitchell were joint winners of the George Devine Award 2000 for Most Promising Playwright for Lift Off and The Force of Change respectively. At the Barclays Theatre Awards 2000 presented by the TMA, Richard Wilson won the Best Director Award for David Gieselmann's Mr Kolpert and Jeremy Herbert won the Best Designer Award for Sarah Kane's 4.48 Psychosis. Gary Mitchell won the Evening Standard's Charles Wintour Award 2000 for Most Promising Playwright for The Force of Change. Stephen Jeffreys' I Just Stopped by to See The Man won an AT&T: On Stage Award 2000.

David Eldridge's Under the Blue Sky won the Time Out Live Award 2001 for Best New Play in the West End. Leo Butler won the George Devine Award 2001 for Most Promising Playwright for Redundant. Roy Williams won the Evening Standard's Charles Wintour Award 2001 for Most Promising Playwright for Clubland. Grae Cleugh won the 2001 Olivier Award for Most Promising Playwright for Fucking Games. Richard Bean was joint winner of the George Devine Award 2002 for Most Promising Playwright for Under the Whaleback. Caryl Churchill won the 2002 Evening Standard Award for Best New Play for A Number. Vassily Sigarev won the 2002 Evening Standard Charles Wintour Award for Most Promising Playwright for Plasticine. Ian MacNeil won the 2002 Evening Standard Award for Best Design for A Number and Plasticine. Peter Gill won the 2002 Critics' Circle Award for Best New Play for The York Realist (English Touring Theatre). Ché Walker won the 2003 George Devine Award for Most Promising Playwright for Flesh Wound.

ROYAL COURT BOOKSHOP

The bookshop offers a wide range of playtexts and theatre books, with over 1,000 titles. Located in the downstairs Bar and Food area, the bookshop is open Monday to Saturday, afternoons and evenings.

Many Royal Court playtexts are available for just £2 including works by Harold Pinter, Caryl Churchill, Rebecca Gilman, Martin Crimp, Sarah Kane, Conor McPherson, Ayub Khan-Din, Timberlake Wertenbaker and Roy Williams.

For information on titles and special events, Email: bookshop@royalcourttheatre.com
Tel: 020 7565 5024

PROGRAMME SUPPORTERS

The Royal Court (English Stage Company Ltd) receives its principal funding from London Arts. It is also supported financially by a wide range of private companies and public bodies and earns the remainder of its income from the box office and its own trading activities.

The Royal Borough of Kensington & Chelsea gives an annual grant to the Royal Court Young Writers' Programme.

The Jerwood Charitable Foundation continues to support new plays by new playwrights through the Jerwood New Playwrights series. Since 1993 A.S.K. Theater Projects and the Skirball Foundation have funded a Playwrights' Programme at the theatre. Bloomberg Mondays, the Royal Court's reduced price ticket scheme, is supported by Bloomberg. Over the past seven years the BBC has supported the Gerald Chapman Fund for directors.

ROYAL COURT

AUTUMN 2003
JERWOOD THEATRE UPSTAIRS

1 September - 4 October
A Royal Court and Told by an Idiot
co-production
PLAYING THE VICTIM
by **the Presnyakov Brothers**
Translated by **Sasha Dugdale**
Directed by Richard Wilson

Cast: Hayley Carmichael, Michael Glenn Murphy, Paul Hunter, Amanda Lawrence, Ferdy Roberts, Andrew Scott.

Design: Nicolai Hart Hansen, Lighting: Colin Grenfell, Sound: Ian Dickinson.

16 October - 15 November
THE SUGAR SYNDROME
by **Lucy Prebble**
Directed by Marianne Elliott

Design: Jonathan Fensom, Lighting: Chris Davey, Sound: Ian Dickinson.

26 November - 10 January
A Royal Court and Out of Joint
co-production
DUCK by **Stella Feehily**
Directed by Max Stafford-Clark

Cast: Gina Moxley, Ruth Negga, Aidan O'Hare, Tony Rohr, Karl Shiels, Elaine Symons.

Design: Jonathan Fensom, Lighting: Johanna Town, Sound: Paul Arditti.

BOX OFFICE 020 7565 5000
www.royalcourttheatre.com

Blood

Characters

Rosa
Eric
Madeleine H
Luca
Claude's voice
Emile's voice
Cameraman
a television crew

Scene One

Rosa *is sitting in an armchair in a brightly lit TV studio; directly opposite her sits* **Madeleine H**, *who is about the same age.* **Rosa** *has short dark hair, is beautiful, in very good physical shape, perhaps a little too thin, dressed in a dark blue suit; seems relaxed, almost indifferent, later chooses her words and expressions with care, economy and ease. We can't quite hear what they are saying yet. They're just making small talk, they're smiling at each other, they seem a little incongruous – perhaps they're talking about the summer, places to go on holiday, perhaps clothes, the weather . . .* **Madeleine H** *offers* **Rosa** *some mineral water;* **Rosa** *asks if it's carbonated, says she doesn't want carbonated mineral water.*

Rosa What's the point of bubbles, you don't need them.

We sense and can also see a number of people busy preparing around them. On the table lies the book **Rosa** *has written, which is the reason for the interview.*

Meanwhile **Eric** *enters the room, he's just changed in his bedroom, he's put on grey jeans, a black T-shirt, a dark blue cashmere sweater; takes a deodorant he's just bought out of a plastic bag, takes off the lid, smells it, pulls a face, thinks it's too sweet, puts some on his wrist. From the same bag he then takes out some books, three CDs, the* 'Goldberg' Variations, *then the* Four Seasons *and then the soundtrack to* Three Colours: Blue – *then he goes and pours himself a glass of wine, disappears, returns, opens a window but there are no sounds from outside; uses the remote control to turn on the CD player as he walks past it – it's Maurizio Pollini playing Schubert's Sonata in D major. He is barefoot. He stops, has a sip of wine, then puts the glass down, fetches another plastic bag, which contains a newly bought jacket that he now takes out, considers trying it on but doesn't; puts it over a chair, looks at it, then forgets about it – goes to the bookshelf, pulls out Cioran's* History and Utopia, *searches for a sentence that he's underlined; then also pulls out Marcus Aurelius'* Meditations, *and* Major Trends in Jewish Mysticism *by Scholem, puts all three books on the big dining table; he looks calm, almost happy; he stays there – he seems slightly restless, it's as if he's vainly trying to remember a sentence that he's forgotten. He uses the remote control, which he* *holds on to during the entire scene, to listen to the answering machine messages, at the same time he turns on the TV, sees the title of the programme* Imago, *and then he hears his own voice; he watches* **Rosa***'s calm face while he listens to his own voice, which is calm, serious, thoughtful. He slowly turns down the Schubert.*

Eric's voice (*answering machine*)   This is Eric Sabato's answering machine. I'm afraid I can't take your call at the moment. If you leave your name and number I'll get back to you later. Please speak after the following tone. Thank you.

Madeleine H (*gives* **Rosa** *a quick smile and then turns to the camera, which is now turned on, and looks into it in a calm and matter-of-fact way, as if it's a colleague*)   Good evening . . . Welcome to *Imago*. Tonight we have the pleasure of welcoming a rare and fascinating guest . . . a woman who, although she is more famous for asking questions than answering them, has kindly agreed to join us this evening. She is the journalist and writer Rosa Sabato. (*Turns to* **Rosa**, *who reappears in the shot.*) Welcome to *Imago*.

Rosa   Thank you.

Madeleine H   Well, we're very grateful and pleased that you're able to come here to talk about your new book . . . Perhaps I should start by saying that for many years you've been praised, both here and abroad, for your reporting from different war zones across the world . . . Beirut, Afghanistan, Guatemala, Angola . . . and now, this winter, for your reporting from the siege in Sarajevo . . . Later in the programme I'd like to come back to the specific difficulties of working as a journalist, as a *female* journalist, in the most hellish places on earth . . . But it's not as one of France's most skilful and brave journalists that you're in the news at the moment, but because you've recently published a . . . should I call it a novel or rather an autobiographical narrative? – which has attracted huge attention and been celebrated as a singularly honest and revealing description of one woman's life under a military dictatorship.

Claude's voice (*answering machine – slowly, with a bad cold*)
Hello . . . It's Claude. I don't think I can come tomorrow.
I've got terrible flu . . . I don't think I'm ever going to get
well again . . . but if I do I'll see you next week.

Madeleine H   Your last book was based on reports from
the war in Guatemala; this is your first novel . . . How did
you come to choose the form of a novel to describe these
events, which as far as I understand are based on facts and
reality? . . . Was it perhaps because this way it was easier for
you to be objective about your fate, or – ?

Rosa   Yes . . . I'd reached a critical point in my life when I
. . . a kind of, well, perhaps emptiness . . . when I felt . . . I
felt a growing need to stop and examine the experiences and
events that made me the person I am today . . . both as an
individual and as a professional . . . to search through the
chaos for the thing that links those crucial memories which
in the end define a life . . . When you've lived under
extreme stress for such a long time and you've had to strain
to understand and describe human and social catastrophes
as I have – you're always on call, it's like working in
casualty, you try to deal with the most important things –
you feel with an increasing sense of powerlessness that
you're pushing yourself to one side, that you don't really
exist any more as a person because you no longer have time
to see how things are affecting you . . . you experience the
gradual erosion of your sense of self . . . And that, after all,
should be your guideline . . . As a journalist you can easily
turn into a machine, you can't hold on to feelings for long,
because if you did you wouldn't be able to carry on . . . but
on the other hand when you try to describe and understand
the suffering, the often meaningless suffering, without any
feelings of your own . . . that's not possible either. I could
have tried to find some way to anaesthetise myself or I could
have become emotionally burnt out, cynical – it's very easy
to stop feeling when you can't change anything . . . or
instead I could decide to actively investigate the
circumstances of my life . . . how the things I've experienced

have shaped who I am . . . like waves make patterns in the
sand at the bottom of the sea . . . I mean – (*laughs*) – being
burnt out is actually a terrible state to be in, one I'd to
anything to avoid. You have to try to look at each new hell
with fresh eyes for as long as you can, so that you can
honestly report its horrors.

Madeleine H   Your book has been described as an
intense novel about the fate of a modern woman in a time of
ruthless social change, and the central section is based on
your own painful experiences in Chile in the seventies . . .
You start by describing your childhood and upbringing in
Santiago de Chile in the fifties and sixties, where you grew
up in a fairly prosperous liberal middle-class home with
European values –

Rosa (*smiles*)   Yes, whatever those are. Classical literature
and music, piano lessons . . . a respect for education and a
liberal view of things in general –

Madeleine H   Yes. You had, I suppose one could say, a
rather harmonious childhood.

Rosa   Yes, very harmonious . . . My father was an
engineer, my mother a doctor . . . I had a happy, sheltered
childhood. I was an only child. I had almost no contact with
people who were less privileged than me. I don't even think
I knew they existed.

Madeleine H   Your father taught at the Institute of
Engineering . . . In the sixties you studied political science at
university and it was there, wasn't it, that you eventually
met your husband and became involved in the socialist
movement of the time, which was active not only in Europe
– well, above all in Paris; here in Paris we remember how
ten million workers demonstrated in the streets and in
factories – but also spread widely across Central and South
America.

Rosa   You could say it was more violently active in
Central and South America, with Castro, Che Guevara –

Madeleine H Yes . . . Che Guevara was a big name in the sixties, a kind of saint . . . Then you became more active in Allende's Popular Front – Salvador Allende, who later became Chile's first democratically elected president.

Emile's voice (*answering machine*) It's Emile. (*Pause.*) I'm sorry I'm phoning when I know you're not home. I'm supposed to be lying on your couch in rue Bonaparte right now. But I'm at home. I've swallowed forty Mogadon and I'm about to fall asleep. (*Pause.*) I just want to say goodbye. (*Pause.*) How do you say goodbye? (*Laughs.*) How do you say goodbye to someone who's done everything in his power to postpone the moment when the one who can't go on any more chooses to give up . . . actually – I promise you – without despair. I simply don't care any more. I'm trying not to throw up. I want to be clean when they find me. (*Pause.*) I know you've been worried although you've tried to hide it. You've helped me enough. Now let me go! (*Pause.*) I would have died a long time ago if it hadn't been for you. (*Pause.*) Eric . . . Eric . . . that's the first time I've called you that . . . Take care . . . Goodbye. (*Laughs again.*) I'm sorry I've wasted your time . . . and mine. (*Short pause.*) Thank you.

Rosa I was nineteen I think when I started working for Allende's democratic alliance. At that time every young person you met was active politically. Politics was the only thing you talked about. You didn't ask what films or music someone liked, but which socialist faction they belonged to, and then you knew who they were . . . I was part of a group that organised classes for people who were really poor, people living on the streets and on the rubbish dumps; we tried to teach them to read and do basic maths . . . The other members were students as well, and we passionately believed then it was possible to change society, to move towards democratic socialism.

Madeleine H So you were a committed socialist . . . Then what do you think about –

Rosa   Well, a socialist . . . in any case I was extremely left
wing. It was like that in those days. There were no other
means. If you were young and susceptible it was easy to be
seduced by socialism, though our beliefs were different from
the reality we know today . . . And we also don't know what
would have happened in Chile . . . if everyone who
embodied a longing for freedom and justice hadn't been
murdered, disappeared or, like me, forced into exile.

Eric *has gone to the phone, dials the same number a couple of times
but keeps getting an engaged tone.*

Madeleine H   Do you think it could have ended like it
did in Cuba or Nicaragua?

Eric *puts down the phone.*

Rosa   Perhaps, probably. (*Without a change in tone.*) I'm sure
I was a fairly clumsy Marxist, without any deep ideological
knowledge . . . What made me get involved was the daily
sight of people drowning in poverty and misery, in a society
based on exploiting most of the population . . . Every day on
the bus to university from where we lived, I saw a hell of
hunger, sickness and degradation . . . It's strange how one
day you suddenly understand something you've seen for a
long time without seeing it . . . Only people from my class
were allowed to study at university . . . We read . . . we read
Fanon, Lacouture, Althusser, Lukács, Mao . . . I don't
remember them all.

Rosa's voice (*answering machine*)   Don't miss me tonight,
nine o'clock on Canal+. I'd feel a bit more confident if I
knew your eyes were watching me . . . I wish I hadn't said
yes . . . I'll hurry home. Love you.

Madeleine H   But although there was great public
enthusiasm for Allende, he failed to solve the underlying
economic problems, and so when Pinochet took over, in
order to save the country from ending up in the same
political chaos as many of its neighbours, the majority of
Chileans supported him, didn't they? We're not going to go

deeper into that . . . but in any case the political climate became considerably harsher, and many of Allende's supporters were rounded up and imprisoned.

Rosa   Yes.

Madeleine H   And you were one of them. Together with your husband you were arrested straight after the coup –

Rosa   Yes, I'm one of thousands of people who were taken to the Estadio Nacional.

Madeleine H   That's one of the images that has become very famous.

Rosa   I've looked for my face in those photographs and never found it, but I was there. We were there for fifty-six days. We were abused, we were cold and hungry and the guards treated us like cattle. Then I was taken to Dawson Island and kept there for seventeen months, my husband and I and thousands of others . . . were interrogated and tortured. (*Smiles.*) So if in no other way than by being tortured I finally became a member of the oppressed. As far as my husband and I were concerned, they were particularly conscientious in their punishment because we were also Jewish.

Luca's voice (*answering machine*)   Hello. It's me. Have you forgotten me? I was almost sure you'd come over yesterday, so I skipped my lectures. But you didn't. It's actually a bit difficult for me to organise my day if I have to spend it waiting for someone who stands me up. I just wanted to tell you that I had the test done today, for your sake. I'll find out in ten days, in case you're worried, but I don't suppose you are – you're so old you're going to die soon anyway. (*Laughs.*) It felt like doing a pregnancy test . . . I love you. (*Pause.*) Even though you're an old man.

Madeleine H (*picks up the book*)   I'd like to come back to your book. It's called *Shadow of Herself.*

Rosa Yes . . . I imagine that many of us who've become refugees and who've made a life in another country, think of ourselves as no more than shadows, we live a kind of shadow life we can't talk about with people in our new homeland because they wouldn't understand . . . we're shadows in our new country . . . and we're left as shadows in the old one where we weren't allowed to live. (*Laughs a little.*) I'm a shadow who speaks French . . . I'm very grateful to my parents that I was well educated and so found emigrating relatively easy – after all, on the surface I stayed within the same cultural sphere . . . but the essential things you can't take with you. And the way the world is today we're just creating more and more refugees. (*Laughs a little again.*) A few years ago I happened to leaf through a history book from the Stalin era, and there was a photograph from some communist celebration in the thirties, when all the members of the Supreme Soviet were assembled in the Kremlin, with Stalin in the middle, to watch some military parade. There was something strange about the photo, I couldn't see what at first, but then I realised there were two or three empty spaces between the dignitaries, as if some people were missing, but behind them, in the empty spaces, you could clearly see shadows of people on the wall, one even had an officer's cap. Of course they were the shadows of members of the Supreme Soviet who had been erased from the photo when they fell from grace . . . That's what it's like for us too, people who fled or were murdered – we've been wiped out but in some places you can still see our shadows.

Luca's voice (*answering machine*) I'm sorry. I'm sorry I was so bitter. I'm just lonely and afraid. I hate feeling abandoned. (*Pause.*) I'm always looking for an epilogue. (*Pause.*) I love you and I'm waiting for you. I'm still young, I've got time. I'll go on waiting till you tell me to stop.

Madeleine H The book is . . . and now we come to a very difficult and delicate subject . . . It's dedicated to your son, who disappeared in 1974.

Eric *turns up the TV.*

Madeleine H   Who you and your husband were forced to leave behind in Chile when you were suddenly deported in . . . er –

Rosa   In October 1974. We came to Paris in October 1974.

Madeleine H   Exactly, in October 1974, when you were deported to France.

Rosa   But we'd already lost contact with him when we were arrested.

Madeleine H   How old was he then?

Rosa   He'd just turned eight.

Madeleine H   There was no way you could take him with you?

Rosa   No. (*Pause.*) We weren't allowed to. (*Short pause.*) He was taken from us when we were arrested.

Madeleine H   And since then, since 197 . . . 3 you haven't seen him.

Rosa   No.

Madeleine H   You know nothing about his fate . . . what happened to him?

Rosa   No . . . Nothing.

Madeleine H   Not where he is or how he is . . . or whether he's even alive?

Rosa   No, nothing. Absolutely nothing. I don't know anything. He was in hospital when we were arrested and my parents went to see him, but they wouldn't even let them in . . . because we . . . didn't exist.

Madeleine H   What do you think might have happened to him?

Rosa   I don't know . . . The last time I saw him was at the end of August 1973. That's twenty years ago . . . So he's grown up now. (*Pause.*) A few years ago when Chile became socially acceptable again and the fascists were forgiven . . . and even applauded – when their project, so to speak, was completed – it's always a matter of time – then they issued a general pardon . . . my husband and I returned to Santiago to try and find him . . . it's the only thing we've lived for . . . but no one had heard anything about him . . . We went to the officials we knew were responsible for his and the other disappearances, but we couldn't get any information whatsoever – not even from the church or the Red Cross. He didn't exist anywhere. It was as if he'd never existed. All they could do was commiserate. So many people have disappeared without a trace . . . everywhere. (*Pause.*) Of course we haven't given up. I'm never going to give up . . . not until I know for sure . . . You can't.

Madeleine H   So you think he's still alive?

Rosa   Yes. I'm sure he's alive . . . But that he doesn't know who he is . . . What else can I be sure about? (*Short pause.*) We know that many children of political prisoners were taken to children's homes run by the military in northern Chile, to be depoliticised, but strangely, although they were usually so terribly scrupulous about filing the records of their crimes, they have no information whatsoever about what happened to our son Paolo.

Madeleine H   That must be an open wound in your life.

Rosa   Yes, yes, it is. It's an open wound . . . It was after our visits to Chile – we've been there eleven times now – that I started to write my book . . . as a kind of conversation with him.

Madeleine H   Let's see . . . here . . . There's a photograph of him here in the book. (*We see a photograph of a seven-year old boy on the screen; he's sitting on a simple chair, with his foot in plaster. He's smiling into the camera.*) There he is.

Rosa   Yes. (*Looks at the picture.*) He was seven then . . . It was taken on the terrace of the children's ward at St

Magdalena Hospital in Santiago . . . His right foot is in
plaster. He was playing with his father and his foot got
caught under a merry-go-round, one of those ones you have
to run round and speed up yourself . . . My husband pushed
too hard . . . it must have hurt dreadfully . . . We'd come to
visit him, my husband took the photograph. Paolo is saying
it itches terribly under the plaster . . . We'd brought fruit
and books . . . He really likes reading . . . It was the end of
August. (*The picture of the son disappears.*) My husband was
working at the Barros Luco Hospital; he'd started a project
for workers with mental health problems . . . I'd started
working as a journalist for *Punto Final.* We were so busy . . .
It was like a miracle we got that last day together . . . It was
one of the last days of freedom. You could feel an enormous
anxiety and tension in the air . . . The inflation was
frightening and the foreign banks were trying to force Chile
to its knees – everyone knew that something was coming . . .
Then, on the eleventh of September, the military coup
happened.

Eric *turns away when the answerphone message comes on, but doesn't
go to pick up the phone.*

Rosa   Yes . . . he's so beautiful.

Madeleine H (*after a short pause*)   It must have been
painful to write about –

Eric*'s voice on the tape finishes.*

Rosa (*interrupts her*)   Yes of course. It was like dragging
myself out of the grave.

Luca's voice (*answering machine*)   It's me again. I'm sorry.
(**Eric** *turns down the TV.*) I'm sorry I'm telling you that I'm
sorry. I know you don't like it . . . But I'm doing it anyway. I
have to do what I want sometimes . . . I just wanted to tell
you that I saw a woman today I thought was her . . . again.
It was at lunchtime. I was sitting in Deux Magots when she
walked past, she was walking quite quickly but she glanced
at me in passing, our eyes met, very briefly, and something

started in her eyes, I don't know what, a kind of surprise, her eyes opened wide and suddenly, just like that, time stood still, it was sublime, you could sense it, every sound died and I heard a voice inside me saying: that's her . . . Then it was over, and without even having stopped she carried on walking, and I got up and started to follow her . . . She went down to Le Marais as if she didn't have anything particular to do and was just shopping in her lunch break – she went into a little shop and tried on a pair of shoes she wasn't sure she liked. (*The call is cut off.*)

Madeleine H   Thank you for taking the time to come here.

Rosa   Thank you.

Madeleine H   Thank you. (*A short pause.*) And now we have a piece about the American artist Barton Lidice Benes, who is part of the new art movement that has developed in New York in the last couple of years – it's a kind of body art in which the artist uses his own body as both material and subject, to show how man and his environment are threatened by Aids and the post-industrial age, and many people have noted its similarity to the religious art that flourished at the end of the Middle Ages. Barton Lidice Benes, who himself contracted Aids a couple of years ago, has attracted considerable attention for his strange, cruel artefacts, in which he often uses his own blood.

Luca's voice (*answering machine*)   She decided they were boring, said thank you and left, then she went into Fnac, and I thought I'm going to lose her in here, but after a while I walked straight into her in the soundtrack section, she was standing there reading the cover of the *Three Colours: Blue* CD, and I didn't know what to say, I just said: That's kitsch. And then I said sorry and left . . . It's not possible. Miracles like that never happen . . . Although I'm sure it will happen just like that – I'll see her walking past when I'm sitting in a café. She was so like the woman I remember, although the woman I remember was a woman who laughed . . . and much younger of course. (*Laughs again, louder.*) They're showing *Savage Nights* for the last time tonight. Since you can't go I'm going by myself . . . but listen, call me later. Otherwise I'll die. (*Laughs.*) Why would it be her? Why would she be in Paris?

Scene Two

Rosa *and* **Eric** *have eaten; they stay at the big table, drinking wine.*

Eric   No, you were wonderful, very good, concrete.

Rosa   I felt so incredibly insecure, I was pretentious and long-winded, I was talking as if my life was a novel –

Eric   Perhaps it was rather awful for a moment, to see the photograph.

Rosa   But wasn't I too tense, too superficial, too eager? . . . I could feel myself sitting there sifting through words I don't normally use . . . I sounded like advertising copy.

Eric   No, no, no . . . Not at all. On the contrary. Shall we have some fruit? (*Wipes his mouth, pours more wine.*) I reacted like an oyster when you squeeze a few drops of lemon on it: I convulsed . . . but then it passed.

Rosa   The whole time I had this sentence in my head that I wanted to say, but I couldn't remember it . . . Sorry, what did you say?

Eric   I haven't looked at it for . . . since we came to Paris. You know how horrible it was developing those pictures . . . No, you didn't sell out and above all you didn't get too personal. You can't get too personal on a programme like that.

Rosa   Wasn't it vulgar to take part . . . to talk about one's own child?

Eric   Not the way you did it.

Rosa   Why haven't you looked at it for twenty years?
That's a long time. (*Short pause.*) When you know so many
people are watching you with blank curiosity, it's so easy to
be seized by an intoxicating longing to touch them . . . by
saying everything . . . as if you'd be forgiven if you said
everything.

Eric   A lot of people do say everything. They've made a
profession out of it.

Rosa (*drinks wine*)   Have you stopped thinking about him?

Eric   How would I do that?

Rosa   I don't know.

Eric   I think about him every day. (*Pause.*) To pull yourself
. . . to pull yourself out of the grave, I think you said. That
was beautifully put.

Rosa   My God! I can still say beautiful things, though
they're not as beautiful as they used to be. Perhaps that's
your fault. (*Lifts her wine glass again, looks into his eyes.*) Anyway
– now it's done, now the grave is empty. I'm smiling at you.

Eric   Yes, and I'm smiling back.

Rosa   Yes, I can see that. (*Lightly.*) As if that were a job as
well. I just couldn't find any shoes I liked.

Eric   No? (*Short pause.*) It was strange to be reminded of
that old project with the mentally ill in Recoleta. It feels like
it happened in another life. Well, it was another life. I don't
know if I carry anything with me from what I was like then.
Of course . . . nearly all psychiatrists start off by practising
on the poorest and worst off so that, once they're skilled,
they can take on middle-class traumas that pay better. I've
got hundreds of photographs and films I haven't developed.
I documented every patient and their behaviour, because in
those days we thought illness was a language we'd one day
be able to decipher, providing we read it in a sufficiently
caring environment . . . Sometimes I think I've kept them

because I want to end up there myself. I suppose it was the most important time of my life.

Rosa   Wasn't that when you met me?

Eric   Patient and society were one. Patient and doctor were one . . . Yes, of course it was.

Rosa   We never saw each other . . . We don't now either. We just talk about what the other one has been up to.

Eric   We see each other every day – talk, eat, sleep . . . and wake up together.

Rosa   Don't you understand what I mean? (*Pause.*) Would we stay together if we didn't have a child that we'd lost?

Eric (*after a pause*)   I don't know. (*Pause.*) What do you think?

Rosa   I don't know. I don't know anything about love.

Eric (*joking*)   Just that it's blind . . . Thank God . . . I don't want to be there the day love can see. (*Pause.*) Tired?

Rosa   Yes, but only because you are – I'm never too tired to want you . . . Is that a new jacket you're wearing?

Eric   Yes. (*Short pause.*) A bit young perhaps.

Rosa   It looks good on you, but I suppose that's the idea. (*Short pause.*) Tomorrow at eleven I have to sign books at Fnac.

Eric   It's Saturday . . . I was thinking of going to see the Hosoe – the one who took photos of Mishima.

Rosa   I see. (*Short pause.*) Couldn't you wait for me? I'd like to experience a few things with you. We could see it together and then maybe walk along the river and have dinner somewhere . . . We've never done things like that . . . things normal people do . . . But perhaps you're used to doing everything on your own.

Eric   No. That sounds good . . . Although you can't really walk along the river nowadays. (*Pause.*) What was the sentence you couldn't remember?

Rosa   I remember it now. I wanted to change the world. I didn't want the world to change me. But it did. (*Pause.*) So what are we going to do about Easter?

Eric   What are we going to do about Easter?

Rosa   You've got time off and so have I.

Eric (*sighs*)   Um . . . Actually I don't know. I'm not sure I have got time off. I'm going to have quite a lot to do with the new analysts taking their exams.

Rosa   And in the summer?

Eric   Yes . . . I don't know.

Rosa   We have to be together this summer because in the autumn . . . I've thought about it, though I haven't decided yet . . . but I think I'm going to stay in Moscow for one more year. I can't give up now.

Eric   Of course you can't.

Rosa   If you asked me to, I would, just like that. (*Holds out her hand, he takes it, she smiles.*) I think we've got a chance now . . . to start living. Perhaps it's because the book has finally come out, come out of me . . . because I'm free . . . as if he'd grown up . . . as if I should let him live his life . . . It feels like we could breathe freely now. Now perhaps we can live, if not exactly happily, then in a compromise with loss. (*Short pause.*) After all, he's twenty-seven! Perhaps he's got children of his own, if he's alive.

Eric   'Await life's end, count no man blest, till free from pain he gains his rest.' Oedipus Rex.

Rosa   That's what I said: not blessed, but perhaps in a compromise with happiness. (*Short pause.*) What do you think he does, what job do you think he's got?

Eric I don't know . . . Anything.

Rosa Perhaps he's an artist . . . or a doctor. . .

Eric Depends if he's forgotten us or not.

Rosa What do you mean?

Eric I don't know. (*Short pause.*) I've got tickets for *Oedipus* next Thursday. Are you free?

Rosa If I'm not I can arrange to be . . . I wish you didn't find it so easy that I'm away for so long.

Eric A year goes by quickly. (*Smiles.*)

Rosa Every year goes by quickly.

Eric And I can come over for a weekend now and then . . . You shouldn't give up now so much is happening there.

Rosa I'm so tired of their wretched suffering.

Eric I understand.

Rosa And there's no hope. They don't believe in anything. They're robbing their own graves. They haven't even got children's songs they can sing because the communists used them all for propaganda. There are a few people who try to help, who teach the illiterate to read and write, the Salvation Army has started doing things in St Petersburg but . . . (*in a different voice.*) I want to do it tonight . . . I can't bear it . . . You can see how I'm feeling . . . I need it . . . And you?

Eric I don't know. One of my patients died on me. He phoned and said goodbye . . . He had Aids, he was almost under 200 T4 and was going blind.

Rosa Then maybe it was for the best.

Eric Yes.

Rosa You can't help everyone. Just me. You don't need to die as well . . . Please.

Eric   I don't know if I can bear it any more.

Rosa   Yes you can . . . if I can bear it, then . . . (*Short pause.*) We haven't done it for almost six months.

Eric   Can't we do something else? . . . it's always so painful.

Rosa   I love the pain. The pain is the only thing that can take me back to the time when I felt something . . . when I was able to feel something. (*Folds her napkin, takes off her necklace.*)

Scene Three

*In **Luca**'s shabby flat in the north of Paris; beaten-up old furniture, sports clothes, books, a computer, a big photograph of Vittorio de Sica in Paris in 1936, a picture of Katharine Hepburn when she was young, a picture of Jean Seberg from* Breathless; *dishes, CDs, folders, paper, notebooks, etc. **Luca** has changed his clothes five times before the doorbell rings and is completely exhausted. He tears open the door. Music, Nina Simone.*

Luca   For God's sake – where the hell have you been! It's quarter past twelve!

Eric   I told you I was coming at twelve.

Luca   If it had been me I would have been here at quarter to.

Eric   Yes, but I'm here now. Don't make a fuss.

Luca   I'm not making a fuss. I'm just nervous.

Eric (*comes in –* **Luca** *walks around nervously*)   I'm here now. (*He's carrying two big bags full of presents.*) Happy birthday.

Luca   Sit down. (*Pulls **Eric** over to one of the dirty chairs, clears away the clothes that are lying on it.*) Sit here. (*Pushes **Eric** into the chair.*)

Eric   Calm down.

Luca   How can I calm down? We've got to get a move on
. . . How long are you staying? (*Pulls* **Eric** *out of the chair*.) No,
sit here instead. You look like a Bacon painting sitting there.
An hour?

Eric (*laughs a little*)   Wait a minute. (*Pulls out a CD. Sofia
Gubajdulina's symphony* Stimmen . . . verstummen.) This is the
new symphony everyone's talking about. There you go.
What is it?

Luca   Nina Simone.

Eric   No, with you.

Luca   Lie on the bed, you might as well . . . Are you giving
me an hour? What can we manage in an hour?

Eric   There's a lot you can do in an hour. (*Pulls out a bottle
of eau de toilette*.) You'll like this.

Luca   Please take your clothes off. (*Holds on to him.*) Take
everything off. That's the only thing I want. (*Hugs and lets go
and hugs him all at the same time.*) Do you want some wine?
We've got an hour. We could split up. Is that what you
want? Should we be friends instead? Father and son?

Eric (*looks at his watch*)   I'll have a taste but I won't drink.
Now open your presents . . . How are you?

Luca   Not as well as you I imagine. (*Fetches the bottle of wine,
takes two glasses, drops one so it breaks –* **Eric** *takes the bottle and the
remaining glass from him, opens the wine, pours some in the glass.*)
Are you going back later?

Eric   I have to . . . Have you been working out?

Luca   Be honest.

Eric   Have you been working out today?

Luca   Do I need to? Am I old and flabby? I'm not as
flabby as you are . . . but then I like used bodies. How much
time do I get? Can I see you tonight?

Eric   I'm working till nine tonight. I'm sorry.

Luca And after that?

Eric I can't.

Luca So you're just here for lunch. I'm your lunch . . .
And who am I supposed to talk to?

Eric Me. (*Pause.*) Go ahead. (*Short pause.*) Sorry.

Luca I've got forty-five minutes – a therapy session . . .
Oh God – how am I going to say everything I don't want to
say in forty-five minutes?

Eric I can't help it being like that at the moment.

Luca Will it get better later?

Eric I think so.

Luca Do you think I'm asking too much? Don't forget
how quickly you get old.

Eric No, no, not at all!

Luca I want to walk with you and spend time with you
like normal lovers do, walk along the river, sit in a park, I
don't even need to hold your hand, I just need to know that
you're there and that you're not going to disappear the next
minute, maybe go and see a film or go to a bar and sit and
talk openly, for hours . . . no holds barred . . . nice normal
conversations, spend some nice normal time together that
doesn't feel like it's stolen from your other life. We haven't
even been to the cinema and we've been together a whole
year!

Eric You can't walk along the river any more . . . I know.
I'm sorry. I want that too . . . There are some more
presents. Open them.

Luca Why? I don't need a dad who hasn't got time for me
and gives me money instead. Thank you . . . What is it?
(*Takes the present.*)

Eric A novel by Thomas Bernhard.

Luca   How depressing. (*Walks up and down in the room, doesn't open the present.*) So you want me to sit here and read while you're fucking her? (*Short pause.*) We did a lung autopsy today. A forty-nine-year-old taxi driver. It smelt of slaughterhouse and nicotine. Are you going to talk to her?

Eric   Yes.

Luca   When?

Eric   Now. Soon. I'm waiting for the right moment, for a moment that's right for both of us.

Luca   Does that exist? And what happens then?

Eric   I don't know . . . She might die.

Luca   You think so? (*Pause.*) You think so? (*Short pause.*) Of what? How?

Eric   I'll talk to her when we're on holiday, when we're relaxed. I'll need the holiday to explain, to dry her tears, to suffer and split up together.

Luca   So I'm alone again this summer. Then what?

Eric   I think she deserves that.

Luca   What about me – what do I deserve?

Eric   That I'm with her when I leave her, even though I'm probably the last person that could or should try to help her. But we've lived together for thirty years, we've lost a country we can't go back to, and we've lost a child we'll never be able to find – we've lived through anticipation and hope and repression together . . . imprisonment and emigration –

Luca   How the hell can I compete with that? And you're not giving me the chance to live through anything together with you . . . apart from death perhaps . . . Aids.

Eric   We're parents of a son who is neither alive nor dead – just missing. I'm her heaven and her hell. I have to leave her in a way that hurts her as little as possible, and at least make her hope I'm there for her so she can keep talking to me, until she decides to stop because she realises it's pointless.

Luca She's so beautiful – she might meet someone tomorrow and be happy. Would that make you unhappy? Do you regret meeting me? Do you regret that day?

Eric No. Of course I do – now and then . . .

Luca You won't regret it when you've got to know me.

Eric On the day we first met we made love in my student flat in Santiago, and afterwards she said: If you ever leave me I'll die like an abandoned animal.

Luca Well, you both belong to a melodramatic generation. You lot say shit like that . . . Isn't it wonderful to be so loved . . . to hold two people's lives in your hand?

Eric We've only known each other six months.

Luca A year.

Eric Six months.

Luca Physically, yes . . . But when I started the analysis I started- or you did, you're the one who seduced me – a relationship with you – the other stuff is just sex. (*Pause.*) I need someone to talk to. (*Starts to laugh.*) I need a therapist. I need you. You're the best analyst there is. A better analyst than lover at any rate . . . There's no analyst I can go to after you. (*Keeps moving around the room – clears away books and paper from the only armchair, pulls* **Eric** *to the window and then back and so on while he's talking.*) Do you want some different music?

Eric You can't live like this.

Luca I can but you can't. You're just visiting the poor. It's easier when you're used to it.

Eric (*calmly*) I know more about poverty than you do.

Luca (*aggressive*)   What do you know? Oh yes, sorry, you know everything. (*The music now only consists of violent drumming and is fairly loud.*) You can go and buy a shirt for fifteen hundred francs without thinking . . . and your wife's summer wardrobe is probably thirty thousand a year.

Eric (*pulls a slight face*)   Turn it down a bit.

Luca   But when you die you won't have any more than those dead babies they find in the lockers at the Gare du Nord . . . Anyway, I don't understand why people keep buying things – every time you buy something it makes you think about death coming to take it away.

Eric   I was just talking about this room.

Luca   I like it here. It's my home. Cherish what you have, because that's all you're going to get.

Eric (*about a steel floor lamp with a small rusty metal lampshade*) That lamp is nice.

Luca   Do you want it?

Eric   No . . . then you wouldn't have any light.

Luca   I don't need to see. I mostly keep my eyes closed. It would look like a skinhead in your flat . . . not that I know what your flat looks like. (*Short pause.*) My whole life has fallen apart but you're living like you did before, just like before . . . right? Nothing's changed in your life. It looks just the same, right? Doesn't it? (*Lights a cigarette, goes up to him, hugs him – they caress and hug each other.*) At least let's lie down. (*Starts to undo the buttons on* **Eric**'s *shirt, pulls off his jacket.*)

Eric   You can't take off my shirt before you've taken off my jacket . . . Should we be doing this? (*Looks around, there are no curtains in front of the windows.*) There are people over there . . . Everyone can see us.

Luca   Just enjoy it. (*Pulls him to the bed, they lie down facing each other.*) Have you resumed your boring relations with her?

Eric   No.

Luca   But you're going to?

Eric   No . . . I don't think so . . . I can't.

Luca   Doesn't she miss it? (*Pause.*) Answer me.

Eric   We work so much. Don't talk about it now. (**Luca** *gets up, turns off the music and puts on a different record.*) Can't you keep still!

Luca   I want you to listen to this.

Eric   I don't want her to die . . . That's all.

Luca   Now listen, listen . . . Do you think she's going to?

The music is Keith Jarrett's 'The Wind'.

Eric   Yes, I do. (*Sits up.*) I have this strange notion that I'll be able to leave her without her noticing. (**Luca** *turns up the music.*) As if I had just died, not met someone else, and a man . . . who's young enough to be her son. (*Short pause.*) I have to give her some hope when I leave her . . . I'm the last man in her life.

Luca   I saw her on TV last night. She's beautiful.

Eric   Yes. Very.

Luca   She doesn't look forty-nine. I couldn't hear everything she said. But she seems cold.

Eric   People can become cold when they lose something.

Luca   I've lost something too.

Eric   So have I.

Luca   You can live with it, unlike us.

Eric   Do you still have nightmares?

Luca   Only when I'm awake . . . That's why I came to you. Who the hell can I go to now?

Eric I'll ask some of my colleagues, but the problem is the good ones are almost impossible to get. (*Short pause.*) Can't you remember anything about your parents . . . what the atmosphere was like, what your room looked like . . . a hug?

Luca You know I can't!

Eric You can of course, but you won't let it out.

Luca That's the same thing, isn't it. My life starts in prison. There was no life before that. The guards give me chocolate and comic books. Donald Duck and Mafalda and at night they rape me. There are three of them. Two are quite nice, young, they laugh all the time and make jokes, but the third, who is older, always cries afterwards and wants me to forgive him. (*Short pause.*) At first I was in a cell with some boys my age. One of their mothers was there as well, and they made him torture her . . . What do you say to that? You who've heard everything?

Eric Of course that's a trauma, a terrible trauma – but a trauma doesn't have to remain a trauma for ever, it can be changed and become an important part of your personality.

Luca I don't give a fuck. I don't give a fuck about my personality. I just want to find my parents. No, that's not right . . . I want to know who they are and where they went. It doesn't matter if they're alive or dead as long as I know their names.

Eric On some level you have to accept the fact that they're dead.

Luca I just want to have a grave. I need to have a grave.

Eric Yes. (*Short pause.*) I understand, it must be terrible for you. (*Sits up.*) I've still got my shoes on. Sorry!

Luca I want to make love . . . It's the only thing that makes me forget.

Eric I can't . . . Not now.

Luca   You needn't be afraid . . . There's one condom left
. . . an American one.

Eric   Have you been with an American?

Luca   What do you want me to do?

Eric   Where?

Luca   Where? What does it matter? (*Short pause.*) Behind
the Russian embassy.

Eric   When? When was this?

Luca   What does it matter? I need some human contact . . .
with someone now and then.

Eric   Who was it? Was it someone you know?

Luca   Of course it wasn't. I don't make love to people I
know. That's boring . . . It was an American soldier,
African-American. I like soldiers. I grew up with them,
remember?

Eric   You've got to be careful.

Luca   I like them because they know what they want . . . I
was completely worn out afterwards. He nearly killed me.
(*Short pause.*) My favourites are the ones that do stuff they
never thought they could do; they're so brutal then.

Eric   You're the one who's being brutal – to yourself.

Luca   That's the most exciting moment, when the
headlights flash across your face, you're paralysed like a
deer, and you don't know what's going to get out of the car.

Eric   You could get infected.

Luca   I could get killed. I'm already infected. (*Short pause.*)
What does it matter?

Eric   What makes you say that?

Luca   Are you scared now?

Eric   No . . . yes, of course I am.

Luca Poor man . . . You have so much to live for. Your wife, your flat and all those poor desperate people you have to calm down . . . We might have two or three romantic years left before it's over.

Eric Well, that's enough.

Luca For you, maybe. (*Pulls him down.*) Devote yourself to me while I'm still warm . . . And then you can scatter my ashes in some secret place. Put them in a shoebox with the others at the Gare du Nord, and then you can move on.

Scene Four

Rosa and **Eric** *are coming home late, they're dressed up.*

Eric (*helps her take off her coat*) What a wonderful production – I'm glad we finally managed to go to the theatre together . . . the traffic makes me so tired though . . . I don't know if I can go on living here.

Rosa Yes . . . I suppose it was.

Eric (*while the coat slips from his fingers*) But then the subject is always interesting, bloody and interesting. I get frightened every time I see him searching for the clues to his own downfall . . . yet somehow not . . . because although he's blinded himself he's also moving towards a more truthful life . . . (*Laughs.*) I identify with all three of them.

Rosa And meanwhile you're getting my coat dirty . . . You've dropped it. (*Points.*) There.

Eric Sorry. (*Picks it up.*) Who did you identify with?

Rosa Who would you like me to identify with? Are you tired?

Eric Mankind . . . But we hardly ever see things that way: stripped bare, as naked as a skeleton – like the production – skeletal. It's only in the theatre that beauty resembles atonement . . . I don't understand why my patients don't cry and scream more.

Rosa   I asked if you're tired.

Eric   Yes, I suppose I am . . . but only deep down. (*Enters the room, turns on the lights.*) No one lives here . . . Do you want a glass of wine?

Rosa   We live here . . . Tired of what?

Eric   It was so short. We've got a whole evening left . . . But the truth is always short.

Rosa   Is that too long for you . . . What will you do with me for all those hours? What are you tired of?

Eric   Just people needing me.

Rosa   Including me?

Eric (*a bit sharp*)   No, of course not. (*He pours wine, hands her the glass.*) How was Fnac?

Rosa   I'd forgotten about that . . . Thanks. (*Remembers.*) We forgot to vote!

Eric   For God's sake . . . who would we vote for? This country is just the sum total of its own neuroses. And we're strangers here, it's not our country. We're only allowed to stay here as long as we don't ask for anything or draw attention to ourselves . . . And that suits me fine.

Rosa (*drinks*)   I must have written my name about 160 times. I forgot how to spell it.

Eric   I feel I've done my bit.

Rosa   I suppose most of them were just passing by, but maybe a few of them will read the book.

Eric   I'm sure they will.

Rosa   When are you going to read it?

Eric   Soon.

Rosa   After all it's about you.

Eric   Is it?

Rosa (*after a long pause*)   The day you realise I love you I'll have the courage to hate you. (*Pause.*) There was a very nice young man who welcomed me and looked after me, he told them when I needed a break and brought me mineral water and fruit. He'd put a rose on the table. I talked to him for a bit afterwards. Italian or Spanish. Spoke a wonderful dark French.

Eric   I see . . . Didn't you ask him where he was from?

Rosa   I was going to, but I forgot. He was just a temp. (*Takes his hand.*) I need you. (*Short pause.*) My body needs you too.

Eric   Yes. (*Sighs and then kisses her cheek.*) You're so beautiful. That colour suits you.

Rosa   Yes, I know . . . Don't you need me? Doesn't your body need me?

Eric   Of course.

Rosa (*after a short pause*)   Do you know what he told me?

Eric   Who?

Rosa   The young Italian or Spaniard at Fnac.

Eric   No . . . What did he tell you?

Rosa   He said he knows you. He said, I know your husband.

Eric   I see . . . How strange . . . What's his name?

Rosa   As a patient. Apparently he was in analysis with you for a while . . . But you stopped the analysis.

Eric   I stopped it? Why?

Rosa   But I'm sure it was my fault, he said.

Eric   Perhaps I hadn't really started it . . . What's his name?

Rosa   I'm telling you I don't know. Hugo, I think. All your patients are called Hugo.

Eric (*short*)   I can't remember. (*Calmer.*) Who is he?

Rosa   I told you! Young, twenty-five, twenty-six, beautiful, Southern European. Very pleasant and articulate. White shirt and leather jacket. Good-looking. Unpretentious or extremely pretentious. Impossible to tell.

Eric   When was this supposed to have been?

Rosa   He said it wasn't your fault you'd stopped the treatment. He thought his problems were so simple they weren't worth your attention.

Eric   Hang on a minute. (*Pause.*) Now I know who you're thinking of. Now I know who you mean . . . Yes, that's right. (*Short pause.*) Some more wine?

Rosa   Yes, it's nice . . . Thank you. (*Pause.*) Why did you stop the analysis?

Eric   Don't think about him now.

Rosa   I'm not thinking about him . . . I just want to know why.

Eric   Well, probably because I didn't think I could help him.

Rosa   With what?

Eric   With what he needed help for.

Rosa   What was that?

Eric   What does it matter?

Rosa   Can't you help everyone?

Eric   I can only give them the chance to search for something of value in themselves – whether it actually exists

or whether they want to search for it they have to decide
themselves. (*Short pause.*) Now I remember . . . He was the
one who had a problem with his foot. He came to see me
because he thought he was losing control. He had suddenly,
without any reason, committed some rather serious acts of
violence against strangers – he'd beaten up an old woman in
a metro station, assaulted a taxi driver . . . things like that.
He was sentenced to a couple of months in prison . . . He
was scared because he'd completely forgotten what he'd
done, and why . . . his childhood as well . . . We got to the
point where he could see that he'd repressed the majority of
his childhood, he knew nothing about his past . . . I think
he'd grown up in a children's home. When you experience a
drastic change of environment as a child you can react by
wiping out both the past, which you've lost, and the present,
which you don't want to live in.

Rosa   How sad.

Eric   I think he was studying medicine . . . It would've
needed a very long, intense period of treatment to get to the
root causes and I can't accept any new patients . . . You
know I want to start cutting down on my cases . . . I've had
enough. (*Short pause.*) He didn't say anything else?

Rosa   Oh, we just exchanged a few words . . . He was so
gentle. I can't imagine he'd be violent . . . he's so polite and
cultivated.

Eric   That's probably how he keeps his aggression at bay.

Rosa   Stop talking now.

Eric   You're the one who's talking.

Rosa (*caresses his thigh*)   What do you want me to do? I
need you. I'm serious.

Eric   Me or it?

Rosa   That's the same thing . . . Don't you want to do it?

Eric   Yes, no, I don't know.

Rosa   You can't be without it either.

Eric   But I don't enjoy it, I suffer.

Rosa   Who suffers the most? Who enjoys the suffering most?

Eric   But is it suffering when it's not really dangerous?

Rosa   It is dangerous. It's always been dangerous. I know you believe that if we can say everything then we can speak the truth – but you must know there are some thoughts we shouldn't think, because they open the gates to hell . . . and then we get used to stepping through them and disappearing. That's what I want. To disappear into your flames.

Eric   Can't we stop this soon? (*Short pause.*) Just stop.

Rosa   We can't. (*Short pause.*) What if it's the only thing that connects us now, the only thing that's left . . . Where would we find anyone else who'd understand?

Eric   There are so many of them . . . More and more every day. Oedipus' children . . . Jocasta's children.

Rosa   Do it now. Come on. You like it when you're doing it.

Eric   You like me when I'm doing it . . . Do I have to?

Rosa   Yes.

Eric *gets up, exits, returns carrying a dirty old steel chair, equipment for tying her up, a rusty floor lamp without a lampshade, a dirty sack, then a mattress with stiff brown leather sheets – sets up the strange room, turns off the lights in the living room, turns on the old lamp, goes up to her while she's sitting there keeping her eyes closed, gently places his hand on her shoulder; she gets up quietly, and with his hand held lightly against her back he guides her into the room, points at the chair, motions her to sit down – she sits down – still with her eyes closed.*

Eric   Open your eyes.

Rosa (*looks up*)   Good.

Eric (*hits her*)   Shut your mouth.

Rosa   I'm sorry.

Eric   I didn't give you permission to speak. (*Kicks her hard, it hurts, she cries out.*) Didn't you hear what I said! Not a word from your filthy lips. (*She drops her head.*) Lift your head up. (*Forces her face up.*) Quickly. (*Friendly.*) How are you?

Rosa   I'm sorry.

Eric   I said: how are you?

Rosa   I don't know.

Eric   You don't know how you are?

Rosa   I'm sorry.

Eric (*still friendly*)   Don't apologise, you little Jewish whore. Just answer my questions. All of my questions. Then you can apologise.

Rosa   Yes.

Eric   So –

Rosa (*quietly*)   The music.

Eric (*grabs her hair, pulls her head back even further*)   Didn't you hear what I said?

Rosa (*feebly, quietly*)   The music . . . you're forgetting the music.

Eric (*slowly twists her hair*)   I'm not forgetting anything. . .

Rosa   No.

Eric   Who's the one forgetting herself? (*Hits her in the face.*)

Rosa   Not my face.

Eric   I'm sorry.

Rosa   I need it.

Eric   What do you need it for? (*Tears open her blouse – it tears, then tears off her bra.*) You like this, don't you? (*She doesn't answer.*) I told you to answer me. I said: you like this.

Rosa   Yes.

Eric   Perhaps you think you're beautiful. It's not true. You're not beautiful. You're too old. We've got beautiful young girls here with firm young breasts – yours are saggy and veined, who'd want those? (*Grabs one of her nipples.*) Like old tyres. Who'd want those? Do you think I want to be here with you? Answer me!

Rosa   No.

Eric   Louder.

Rosa   No.

Eric   Well you're right. But we can do this the easy way or the hard way, can't we? (*Pause.*) How do you want it? Do you want it the easy way or the hard way, you saggy Jewish cunt?

Rosa   Yes.

Eric   You can tell me the truth or not. I don't care. You mean nothing. It doesn't matter if you're alive or dead. You never existed. (*Pulls the dirty sack over her head.*) What's your name? What was your name before you came here? (*She says something.*) Louder!

Rosa   Sabato. (*Short pause.*) Rosa Sabato.

Eric   Were you Jewish?

Rosa   Yes.

Eric   So what are you now? (*Goes to the CD player, puts on a tape with ducks that chatter a lot, sometimes fairly loudly, at times it sounds like a song.*) Was everyone in the group Jewish?

Rosa   I don't know . . . it wasn't a group . . . we were just students.

Eric *hits her.*

Scene Five

Eric *is tidying up the flat, listening to music and preparing to work. The entryphone rings. He goes and picks it up.*

Eric Yes? Hello?

Luca (*upset*) I have to see you! Open the door! Hurry!

Eric No, I can't . . . I can't. (*Short pause.*) Go away.

Luca I have to see you!

Eric You can't come here. You must see that. (*Short pause.*) Luca. Go home.

Luca Let me in – it's important. I have to see you now!

Eric Rosa could be here any minute . . . don't you understand? It's impossible.

Luca Open the door.

Eric I can't. It's impossible. I'll phone you. (*Hangs up, stays by the entryphone, it rings again.*)

Luca (*when* **Eric** *answers*) I might be HIV-positive . . . What are you going to do then?

Eric No you're not.

Luca What are you going to do then? What are you going to do?

Eric Please . . . I can't talk about it on an intercom.

Luca That's the only choice you're giving me! (*Pause.*) Isn't it? (*Pause.*) Hello!

Eric Yes . . . I'm here, but I can't talk long.

Luca Go to hell. (*Pause.*) Open the door. Open it now.

Eric I can't talk now. I'll come to your place . . . (*Looks at his watch.*) In three hours. (*Pause.*) Hello . . . I'll come in three hours. (*Silence.*) Luca. (*Listens.*) Luca . . . Answer me. (*Silence.*) Luca – I know you're there. Hello . . . Now answer me.

(*Stands there for a while, then hangs up the phone, then picks it up again.*) I know you're there. Now go home and wait . . . I'll come in three hours. At nine . . . Then we'll talk. (*Silence, he hangs up, goes back into the room, he's very worried, goes to his desk, sits down, gets up. The doorbell rings. He runs out into the hall, tears open the door.*) What!

Luca (*calmly*)   I want to see you. I just want to see you. It's all right.

Eric (*after a pause*)   Go. (*Pause.*) I'm begging you.

Luca   I just want to see how you live, what it's like. (*Smiles.*) I was worried about you.

Eric   Now go. She could be home any minute. Don't you understand?

Luca   Perhaps that'd be just as well. It can't be good for you to have to lie all the time, both to her and to me. (*Enters the flat.*) Yes, that's exactly how I imagined it would look. So tasteful, so clean, sterile . . . inhuman. The two of you could live here for ever . . . Happy ever after in this sarcophagus. You know, the first time I went to the Uffizi in Florence I thought those big coffins were bathtubs.

Eric   Luca. I'm begging you.

Luca   That's nice – you begging me. Usually I'm the one that does the begging. Why did you give me Thomas Bernhard? It's all about suicide . . . Do you want me to kill myself? Is that your master plan? (*Walks round the room, tears down things, pulls down the CD rack, pulls out books, throws them around, etc, tramples on them.*)

Eric   Stop it. Calm down.

Luca   Why don't you calm me down! You're the therapist! You know how to calm people down! (*Pushes him.*) Go on! Do some therapy on me!

Eric (*calmly*)   What do you want?

Luca   What do I want? I've forgotten. I wanted you to accept me. I wanted you to live with me. (*Tries to hug* **Eric**.)

Eric (*pushes him*)   You can't stay here.

Luca *starts to take his clothes off, takes off his shirt, then his trousers, his socks; sits on a chair by the desk which is by an open window, lights a cigarette and then puts his head on the desk, stays still.*

Eric (*who has been trying to stop him*)   What is this?

Luca   Take your clothes off . . . I'm staying here.

Eric   Go away! (*Pulls the chair away from him, hits him.*) Take your clothes and get out.

Luca *laughs.*

Eric   Get out! Get out! Get out! Leave! Go away!

Eric *drags him through the room.* **Luca**, *laughing, tries to fight back.* **Eric** *throws him into the hall, gets his clothes, throws them out the door and then tries to push* **Luca** *out the same way.* **Luca** *just laughs.*

Luca   You are angry . . . I didn't think you could get this angry!

Eric   Get up and go.

Luca   Oh shit.

Eric   Get out.

Luca   I can't . . . I can't walk. It's my foot. I can't stand on it.

Eric   You have to leave now. (*Calmer.*) I'm sorry. I didn't mean to hurt you.

Luca   I can't put any weight on my foot.

Eric   Put your clothes on and go downstairs and I'll call a taxi.

Luca   It's not your fault. I'm always hurting my right foot. I've broken it several times . . . Do you know – the last

memory I have of my parents is when I'm in hospital
because I've broken it, I don't know how, and they've come
to see me. (*Gets up slowly, puts his weight on his left foot, holds on to
a chair.*) They've brought me some fruit and books. I think
it's Sunday because the bells keep ringing, and the weather
is beautiful, and they push me out on to a terrace. It was *The
Three Musketeers* . . . I never got to finish it. That's my last
memory of them. Then they were gone. (*Tries to hug and kiss*
Eric.) I'm sorry but I got the result today. I'm positive. I'm
really scared.

Eric (*moves back, frightened*)   No.

Luca   It'll pass.

Eric   It's not true.

Luca   Yes. It's true. Last night I dreamt I got a letter
saying I was positive. I was so happy when I realised it was
just a dream. Then I had a couple of lectures and when I
got back in the afternoon there was a letter from the
hospital.

Scene Six

Luca's flat. He's restless, can't sit still; goes to the phone; calls **Eric**,
hangs up; puts on some music, turns it off, goes to the wardrobe,
searches through his clothes; throws himself down on the bed; calms
down; decides to get dressed and go out. The doorbell rings. **Luca** is
happy, runs to the door thinking it's **Eric**; is happy and angry at the
same time.

Luca   So there you are! (*Opens the door.*)

Rosa (*standing outside*)   I'm sorry . . . I'm sorry to disturb
you this late. I don't know if you remember me. I saw you
on the metro and I thought . . . But perhaps you're –

Luca (*suddenly polite*)   Forgive me . . . Of course I remember
you. Oh yes, of course . . . I didn't know . . . Won't you
come in? It's a bit of mess in here . . . I'm . . . studying . . .

I'm going to be a doctor, I think I told you that at Fnac, but . . . so I haven't got time to . . . or the money – but come in. . .

Rosa   Thank you. I was just going to . . . I don't know why I . . . Well, to be honest I had this impulse and. . .

Luca   That's nice . . . I love it when people follow their impulses . . . Break out of their prisons . . . not that I'm trying to say that you're in some kind of prison –

Rosa   No, I think I probably am . . .

Luca   Well, come in . . . I'll find something to sit on . . . Living in Paris you never think you're going to bump into someone you don't really know . . . Someone you've been thinking about, though I could equally well say the exact opposite – it's only in Paris that you can bump into someone you don't really know but who you've been thinking about . . . Do you live near here?

Rosa   No, no.

Luca   Do you live in the middle of Paris?

Rosa   Sort of . . . You have to.

Luca   The eighth?

Rosa   No. That's Champs-Élysées. (*Laughs a little.*)

Luca (*who has lit a cigarette, waves away the smoke*)   I'm sorry . . . Do you mind – ? (*Puts it out.*) Yes. . .

Rosa   No, no . . . Go ahead and smoke . . . Do you live alone?

Luca   Yes . . . no. I'm with people all the time; I like being completely alone among people. I dissected someone today. (*Short pause.*) At first I turned my face away when I had to cut him open, but the pathologist said you'll get used to it . . . and it's true . . . (*She looks at him, he meets her gaze, smiles quickly, then turns his face away, looks down.*) Well . . . You're married . . . Of course, your husband . . . What did he say? (*Laughs.*) Did

he remember me . . . or my symptoms . . . Can he
remember a man who can't remember?

Rosa   Yes . . . Of course. (*Short pause.*) I don't really know
why I came here. . .

Luca   No, but you wish it would happen more often, don't
you? (*Gets up.*) That you meet someone and . . . you don't
have to explain anything. And then . . . Don't you want to
stand up?

Rosa *stands up.*

Luca *hugs her, kisses her.*

Rosa   And then?

Luca *unbuttons her blouse, caresses her breasts. They undress each
other. They make love. Then they lie side by side, holding hands. They
don't look at each other.*

Luca (*after a while, smiles*)   Do you smoke after you've made
love?

Rosa   I never smoke . . . But you go ahead if you feel like
it.

Luca   No, I don't feel like it. (*Pause.*) I'm totally satisfied.
(*Longer pause.*) Have you seen the new Chéreau film – *La
Reine Margot*?

Rosa   No, no, nothing . . . There's so much I haven't seen.

Luca   The critics were completely baffled by it . . . There's
a fantastic scene at the end when the Queen Mother, Virna
Lisi, burns her underwear. She's got syphilis. She's rotting
from the inside. Her face has turned into a cranium . . .
Adjani plays Margot.

Rosa   Yes. I must see it. I'll try and see it.

Luca   Yes. But you can't see everything. (*Pause.*) Did you
like it?

Rosa   Yes. I think so.

Luca   But of course it depends what your motive was . . . doesn't it?

Rosa   What was my motive?

Luca   The same as mine, perhaps. (*Pause.*) Revenge?

Rosa   I've never done anything like this before. (*Short pause.*) Where are you from?

Luca (*short pause*)   Why? I'm not French?

Rosa   No. Don't be offended. (*Pause.*) You're not, are you?

Luca   I'm not? Then what am I? (*Sits up, looks at her.*) Do you want something to drink?

Rosa   No. (*Sits up as well, glances around looking for her clothes.*) Spain?

Luca   Spain? No. Not Spain.

Rosa (*after a pause*)   It could be anywhere.

Luca   Yes . . . anywhere. (*Gets up, goes and fetches her bra, returns, hands it to her; she is sitting like a little girl with her hands between her thighs.*)

Rosa   Putting your clothes back on for the first time is almost more embarrassing than taking them off.

Luca (*who is about to put on his socks*)   Did you sleep with me because I was one of your husband's patients?

Rosa (*starts to laugh*)   No, definitely not – I don't think so. (*Catches sight of his injured foot.*) What's that? What have you done to your foot?

Luca   I saw you on TV the other day when you were being interviewed . . . I thought you were really beautiful but I couldn't hear what you said, the sound on my TV goes after a while.

Rosa   What's happened to your foot?

Luca It's nothing . . . I broke it when I was young and I suppose it wasn't looked after properly.

Rosa How? (*Pause.*) What happened? (*Louder.*) How did it happen?

Luca What is it?

Rosa How long . . . how long have you lived in Paris?

Luca Well . . . I've lived here . . . I came here in '89, in the spring. (*Lights a cigarette.*) I'm studying medicine. I'm going to be a doctor. I've been studying for two and a half years now. I want to be a GP . . . meet normal people.

Rosa Who are you? (*After a short pause.*) Are your parents alive?

Luca My parents? Yes . . . I hope so . . . I mean, I didn't have much contact with them last year. It's so far away. My dad's an underwriter for an American insurance company in Santiago.

Rosa American?

Luca He's fifty-eight. He's started to talk about retiring. We haven't got much in common . . . like most fathers and sons. He loves football, works out all the time . . . likes spending time in the mountains, fishing . . . that sort of thing. He's adopted an American lifestyle. My mother's a teacher. I haven't got any brothers or sisters. (*Looks at her.*) What is it? Are you all right?

Rosa Yes . . . I am. . .

Luca Though actually they're my foster parents . . . I'm adopted. . .

Rosa (*after a long pause, quietly, barely audible*)   And the other ones . . . the other ones. . .

Luca Who?

Rosa Your real parents . . . where are –

Luca   They're not particularly real. Just biological . . .
He's right wing, admires Pinochet. If he was American he'd
vote for Ross Perot.

Rosa   Where are they . . . ? What happened to them . . . ?
What do you know – ?

Luca   My biological ones? (*Pause.*) I don't know. (*Lightly.*)
Dead, perhaps. They were so young. They disappeared
during the military coup. They were socialists. (*Lights a
cigarette.*) You probably know all about that.

Rosa   No . . . No.

Luca   I was about six or seven when it happened . . . I'd
just started school . . . I've only got a distant memory of two
beautiful dark figures . . . She was so cheerful and lively . . .
short dark hair.

Rosa   No. (*Long pause.*) No.

Luca (*who has almost finished getting dressed*)   But those things
happened . . .

They hear the door opening. **Luca***'s reaction is one of dismay.* **Rosa**
sits immobile, paralysed on the bed. **Eric** *enters.*

Scene Seven

Eric *comes in through the door, with the key still in his hand – the
room is dark. He says* 'Luca?' *– then catches sight first of* **Rosa**,
*who is still sitting on the bed with her head down, her eyes vacant,
wringing her hands.* **Luca** *is standing in the middle of the room with
the same expression frozen on his face as just before the door opened – a
mixture of surprise and malice and expectation.* **Eric** *looks at* **Luca**
who looks at **Rosa** *who doesn't want to see either of them. Then*
Eric *looks at the key in his hand, grips it tightly, and looks away. A
long silence.*

Luca   Well . . . what can we say? (*Short pause.*) What do you
usually say in a situation like this . . . You could say it's

fucking rude to come bursting in like this without any
notice, but that's the risk intruders always run . . . isn't it?
But maybe it's just as well. The truth will out, sooner or
later. Rather late in this case . . . Honesty is the best policy.
(*Laughs.*) I don't know whether I should offer you anything
when I've just fucked your wife . . . The three of us have so
much in common, it's a shame we have to meet like this, in
this dump . . . But I suppose it's like Bourdieu said, forgive
me for quoting him, our biggest problem is we've ended up
in the wrong place – it's no longer the *condition humaine* but
the *position humaine* that tortures us . . . Is it getting cold? (*To*
Rosa.) Are you cold? Sorry, the concierge drinks, so does
her husband, they never go out . . . You know what it's like.
There's probably no point in talking about it; it would take
so long – betrayal, bad conscience, filth, repetition,
acceptance. It's happened now. You'd be better off joining
the family therapy centre or doing something for heroin
addicts from North Africa.

Rosa *gets dressed.* **Eric** *avoids looking at her.* **Luca** *wants to help
her out of politeness but she doesn't react – she gets up, walks around,
stops in front of a photograph of* **Eric** *that shows him standing in a
square in Florence.*

Rosa I took that last summer in Florence. (*Short pause.*) I
haven't seen it before.

Luca I went there for a week hoping that we'd suddenly,
through sheer coincidence, bump into each other
somewhere and perhaps go and have an espresso . . . It's
nice, isn't it? (*Short pause.*) It's a happy picture.

Rosa We talked about going back there this summer, a
couple of weeks . . . To the same place.

Luca It's a pity that the first time we meet it has to be like
this, but . . . these things happen.

Rosa (*doesn't turn around*) It's not the first time.

Luca What?

Rosa (*whispering*)   It's not the first time.

Luca   I mean the three of us. It's the first time we've all met.

Rosa   We've met before.

Luca   I see . . . Where? (*Aggressive, to* **Eric**.) Sit down, move, do something! (*In a different tone.*) I don't remember that. Where?

Rosa (*looks at him, then at* **Eric** *for the first time*)   You're my son.

Luca   What? (*Smiles.*)

Rosa   You're my son, our son. You're our son. You're Paolo, our son. The last time I saw you was in the hospital in 1973. You were seven years old. It was a Sunday. You were there because you'd broken your foot and Eric and I came to see you. It was a Sunday. We brought books and fruit . . . because you liked reading . . . We sat on the terrace. It was a Sunday.

Luca   You've already said that.

Rosa   That was the last time I saw you.

Luca   No. No. (*Laughs.*) Not me.

Rosa   That was the last time I saw you.

Luca   No, no, that wasn't me. It can't have been me. (*Short pause.*) What book? What book? What books!

Rosa   It's true.

Luca   What books were they?

Rosa   It's true.

Eric   Yes.

Luca   I see . . . (*Short pause.*) And what are you going to do now?

Eric   I don't know . . . I didn't know . . . I wasn't to know.

Luca That's no excuse. . .

Rosa How will you live with this? . . . We?

Eric (*shouts for the first time*) I can't!

Luca What about me? What's going to happen to me . . . with parents like this? It's not true . . . I'll never be able to see anyone . . . how can I face other people and tell them . . . about my parents.

Eric I didn't know . . . How could I . . . how could I . . .

Rosa No.

Eric He was just a patient . . . anybody. . .

Rosa I can't stay here. (*Sits down.*) It feels like I'm losing all my blood.

Luca That must be terrible . . . that must be a terrible feeling.

Rosa (*gets up again, looks around like she's searching for a door.*) I want to leave.

Luca (*calmly*) There's nowhere to go is there.

Eric (*to himself*) Is it a crime if you don't know you've committed it?

Luca (*to* **Rosa**) Calm down . . . Sit down again . . .

Eric Either we have to . . . stay together and help each other . . . or just walk away . . . in different directions, and never see one another again.

Rosa My husband and my son . . . my husband and my son . . . my husband and my son . . .

Eric I didn't know what I was doing.

Rosa My husband and my son, my husband and my son.

Eric What about you? (*Pause.*) We can't talk about this . . . do you see?

Rosa Then what are we going to do?

Epilogue

A cell for two people; quite pleasant; half the cell is occupied by a TV crew preparing for an interview; **Luca** *is sitting on a chair, smiling politely, seems humble, calm, without any strong emotions, at ease in his mind. In the cell are books, toiletries, a transistor radio, two beds; we can see a normal-sized window with bars – we can't see the view outside but it feels banal, walled-in.* **Luca** *is wearing his own clothes – a shirt, trousers, summer shoes. In the corner behind* **Madeleine H** *stands the* **Cameraman**, *who is holding a video camera, also a sound technician, a researcher – all of them are calm and friendly. The* **Cameraman** *is smoking.*

Madeleine H (*to the* **Cameraman**)   Well, when you're ready we can start.

Cameraman   We're ready. (*Short pause.*) There's just one little thing.

Madeleine H   OK, thank you. (*To* **Luca**.) They always make you wait. (*Short pause.*) It looks like we're nearly there.

Luca   It's all right. I don't mind waiting.

Madeleine H   I suppose that's what one does here?

Luca   Yes, sort of . . . Do I look pale?

Madeleine H (*sympathetically*)   Aaah . . . no, I don't think so . . . But it wouldn't be surprising, would it? (*Short pause.*) We didn't get much sun this autumn.

Luca   No, it's a pity . . . But it doesn't matter.

Cameraman   If you're ready, we can. . .

Madeleine H   OK. (*Quickly powders her face.*) Thanks, I'm ready. (*To* **Luca**.) I'll sit here . . . Then we'll record me later. OK. (*Pause.*) We can start then . . . I'll start with a short introduction . . . And then we'll do the interview. Take your time. (*Smiles at him – the camera is running.*) Welcome to *Imago.* We've come to the Department of Forensic Psychiatry at the Salpétrière in order to speak to twenty-seven-year-old Luca

Sabato, who, for the past couple of months, has been examined here after having killed his parents, a murder which has attracted a great deal of media and public attention.

The reason why today's *Imago* programme examines such a harrowing subject, which at first glance doesn't seem to belong in a programme about art and culture, is because this case has been cited as an example of how the borders between life and art have been demolished; it has also breathed new life into the old discussion about authenticity in art and provoked a violent debate about the depiction of such upsetting events, since there are now plans for a film based on the murders. Is the artist responsible for the subjects he chooses to depict, and is he also responsible for how his work affects us . . .

To give you a brief summary of the Sabato tragedy . . . about a year ago Luca Sabato's parents were found murdered in his flat in the eighteenth arrondissement and Luca was immediately the chief suspect. He was arrested and confessed to the crime at once. After his trial he was brought here and is now waiting to receive his sentence . . . The story has obvious parallels with Greek tragedy. It has been described as a modern Oedipus tragedy, not least because those involved only became aware of the connection between them at the very end. Eric and Rosa Sabato were Chilean exiles, who because of their political activities in the sixties were deported from their country and forced to leave behind their young son, knowing nothing about his fate. Their son grew up with foster-parents. Twenty years later all three were reunited in Paris, in an encounter that was to have horrific consequences. Meanwhile, in Paris this year we've had the opportunity of seeing no less than six productions of *Oedipus Rex*, in both historical and modern interpretations . . . Is this merely a coincidence? Have the terrible, cruel events that we're surrounded by – the former Yugoslavia, the conflicts in the Middle East, the wars in Africa, the violence in modern cities – somehow torn off our mask of civilisation? Are we in the middle of a social nightmare and will we see even more examples of these Greek tragedies, has man not progressed at all, is every generation compelled to re-enact the same tragedy, and is it the artist's task to find and shape this tragedy from a stream of inexplicable actions? (*Turns to* **Luca**.) Luca . . . have you yourself been struck by the parallel to the famous Greek tragedy?

Luca (*smiling, aware of his beauty and of his situation*)   Yes, of course. Certainly. Absolutely. On several levels. Except that unlike Oedipus I didn't blind myself. I wanted to see my fate, and my victims . . . I mean, on another level, the whole of South America is one colossal Oedipal tragedy where the corpses of the fathers are stacked one on top of the other . . . Sons and fathers keep murdering each other in the name of social revolutions – on such a large scale that all individuality is lost – those are collective Oedipal tragedies. (*Quick pause, smiles again.*) But that hasn't been any comfort to me. It wasn't until I found out, that I could see it . . . Even my foot . . . Oedipus had a broken foot as well.

Madeleine H   Which of the murders do you think is the most . . . serious? Which upsets you most – the murder of your father or of your mother?

Luca (*after a short pause*)   Well . . . that's an unexpected question . . . I thought I'd heard them all . . . I haven't thought about it . . . I don't know . . . I can't really tell them apart now . . . I knew my father a bit better, but . . . perhaps it's a worse crime to murder your mother . . . certainly here in prison.

Madeleine H   Could you describe your feelings about what happened?

Luca   No. (*Pause.*) I don't know what feelings one could have.

Madeleine H   But . . .

Luca   Do you mean remorse, that sort of thing? . . . Yes. It's difficult to describe. I just see it as . . . as the end of something, as the end of a chain of events that I couldn't influence, that somehow I couldn't prevent . . . as if I didn't have a choice . . . as if I was fulfilling my own destiny.

Madeleine H   In what way?

Luca   But perhaps all murders are . . . seem like . . . I don't know. (*Short pause.*) It's difficult to explain. There was so much happening all at once. I didn't know them . . . Well, Eric, my father – I still find it a bit difficult to call him 'father' – of course, as I said, I knew him a bit better, but Rosa I'd only met twice before it happened. . .

Madeleine H   How come . . . why was she there? Why did she come to your flat?

Luca   She came to see me. She came there. I hadn't expected her to come at all. She just came. She followed me . . . It was so stupid . . . If she hadn't come there it would never have happened. I'd met her in a bookshop about a week before, it was a complete coincidence . . . And then she came to my flat. . .

Madeleine H   And what happened then?

Luca   Well, I've already talked about that.

Madeleine H   What happened then?

Luca   She was very nice. (*Short pause.*) Yes. Not at all like some Greek . . . some Greek apparition.

Madeleine H   Just a normal desperate woman.

Luca   Yes. That's right . . . (*After a short pause.*) Not at first, but then . . . when she said I was her son, but Eric was already there by then – he came later.

Madeleine H   So she said that she was your mother?

Luca   Yes, that's right. (*Short pause.*) Of course I got very upset and –

Madeleine H   Did you think it was true, that she was your mother?

Luca   Yes. Immediately. I don't know why, but I believed it. I believed her . . . As soon as I realised . . . And then when Eric . . . my father . . . came in, and he had the key, it was obvious . . . That's when it came out . . . But I think she knew before then, a little bit before.

Madeleine H   What was it that came out?

Luca   Well . . . the relationship.

Madeleine H (*after a pause*)   The relationship between you and your father? The physical relationship?

Luca   Yes. (*Short pause.*) Yes.

Madeleine H   You were having a physical relationship?

Luca   Yes. (*Short pause.*) That's right.

Madeleine H   A love affair.

Luca   Yes . . . I've talked about it so much with the psychologists here, but I haven't . . . (*Pause.*) Oedipus didn't have an affair with his father, did he?

Madeleine H   No . . . no, I don't think so. (*Pause.*) And then . . . what happened then?

Luca   Well . . . We talked for a bit. And then I killed them.

Madeleine H   Did you know who they were at that point, that they were your father and mother?

Luca   Yes. (*Short pause.*) That's right . . . But that's not why I did it, I did it because . . . I've thought about it . . . I've tried to think about it . . . I've talked about them . . . but I did it . . . actually I did it to help them.

Madeleine H   Help?

Luca   Yes. (*Short pause.*) To spare them. So they wouldn't have to live with what had happened. Yes. It seemed natural, there was nothing else I could do – I couldn't say: OK, bye-bye, let's not see each other again . . . I couldn't carry on living like I did before either, but I did it mainly for them . . . She was first. It was difficult because she didn't die straight away . . . And the knife cut straight across her throat again. Then it was over. (*Short pause.*) That was the first time I've understood the expression from ear to ear. (*He feels like laughing but doesn't.*) And then it was his turn. He wasn't meant to see it, see what she looked like . . . That wasn't the idea. It was meant to be quick so he wouldn't have time to see it . . . Then he died too. (*Short pause.*) And afterwards I was really tired. It felt like I'd driven a car for several days without any rest. I was really tired, completely exhausted. I just collapsed. I fell asleep there. I slept till the next day, till lunchtime, and then I woke up and I was hungry, so I went out to get something to eat . . . I walked around for several days, all over the place; I can't remember where I was or what I did. I didn't want to go back and see them again. I knew what I'd done, but I couldn't think about it, I didn't think about it. It was like a dream, like it was someone else.

Madeleine H   And now? (*Short pause.*) What would you say to them if you met them today?

Luca   Today? (*Pause.*) I don't know . . . I don't know . . . What would I say?

Madeleine H   Do you think they would forgive you?

Luca   No . . . I don't know. (*Pause.*) If anyone would, I suppose it would be them . . . but . . . I don't know.

Madeleine H (*after a long pause*)   Thank you. (*Short pause, then she turns to the* **Cameraman**, *nods, he nods as well.*)

Luca (*breaks the silence*)   Was that good? Was it OK?

Madeleine H   Yes, I think so . . . I think it was good. (*Short pause.*) Do you know when they start shooting the film?

Luca   In May, I think . . . But they want to make some changes to the way I met Rosa – set it in a cafe . . . She's supposed see me riding up on some big old motorbike, I'm wearing a dark suit, a dress shirt and so on, I've been working in some restaurant, and then she comes out and there's supposed to be something going on between her and me . . . but the evening I met her I'd been at the hospital, at an autopsy . . . and then afterwards I'm supposed to ride around Paris on my motorbike, but I've told them to tell it like it was, I want it to be like it was, I don't want them to change anything.

Methuen Modern Plays

include work by

Jean Anouilh
John Arden
Margaretta D'Arcy
Peter Barnes
Sebastian Barry
Brendan Behan
Dermot Bolger
Edward Bond
Bertolt Brecht
Howard Brenton
Anthony Burgess
Simon Burke
Jim Cartwright
Caryl Churchill
Noël Coward
Lucinda Coxon
Sarah Daniels
Nick Darke
Nick Dear
Shelagh Delaney
David Edgar
David Eldridge
Dario Fo
Michael Frayn
John Godber
Paul Godfrey
David Greig
John Guare
Peter Handke
David Harrower
Jonathan Harvey
Iain Heggie
Declan Hughes
Terry Johnson
Sarah Kane
Charlotte Keatley
Barrie Keeffe
Howard Korder

Robert Lepage
Doug Lucie
Martin McDonagh
John McGrath
Terrence McNally
David Mamet
Patrick Marber
Arthur Miller
Mtwa, Ngema & Simon
Tom Murphy
Phyllis Nagy
Peter Nichols
Joseph O'Connor
Joe Orton
Louise Page
Joe Penhall
Luigi Pirandello
Stephen Poliakoff
Franca Rame
Mark Ravenhill
Philip Ridley
Reginald Rose
Willy Russell
Jean-Paul Sartre
Sam Shepard
Wole Soyinka
Shelagh Stephenson
Peter Straughan
C. P. Taylor
Theatre de Complicite
Theatre Workshop
Sue Townsend
Judy Upton
Timberlake Wertenbaker
Roy Williams
Snoo Wilson
Victoria Wood

Methuen Contemporary Dramatists
include

John Arden (two volumes)
Arden & D'Arcy
Peter Barnes (three volumes)
Sebastian Barry
Dermot Bolger
Edward Bond (six volumes)
Howard Brenton
  (two volumes)
Richard Cameron
Jim Cartwright
Caryl Churchill (two volumes)
Sarah Daniels (two volumes)
Nick Darke
David Edgar (three volumes)
Ben Elton
Dario Fo (two volumes)
Michael Frayn (three volumes)
David Greig
John Godber (two volumes)
Paul Godfrey
John Guare
Lee Hall
Peter Handke
Jonathan Harvey
  (two volumes)
Declan Hughes
Terry Johnson (two volumes)
Sarah Kane
Barrie Keefe
Bernard-Marie Koltès
David Lan
Bryony Lavery
Deborah Levy
Doug Lucie

David Mamet (four volumes)
Martin McDonagh
Duncan McLean
Anthony Minghella
  (two volumes)
Tom Murphy (four volumes)
Phyllis Nagy
Anthony Neilsen
Philip Osment
Louise Page
Stewart Parker (two volumes)
Joe Penhall
Stephen Poliakoff
  (three volumes)
David Rabe
Mark Ravenhill
Christina Reid
Philip Ridley
Willy Russell
Eric-Emmanuel Schmitt
Ntozake Shange
Sam Shepard (two volumes)
Shelagh Stephenson
Wole Soyinka (two volumes)
David Storey (three volumes)
Sue Townsend
Judy Upton
Michel Vinaver
  (two volumes)
Arnold Wesker (two volumes)
Michael Wilcox
Roy Williams
Snoo Wilson (two volumes)
David Wood (two volumes)
Victoria Wood

For a complete catalogue of Methuen Drama titles
write to:

Methuen Drama
215 Vauxhall Bridge Road
London SW1V 1EJ

or you can visit our website at:

www.methuen.co.uk